THE ROAD TO MECCA

Also by Athol Fugard

Autobiography
NOTEBOOKS 1960–1977
(edited by Mary Benson)

Plays
(published by Oxford University Press)
STATEMENTS
(Sizwe Bansi is Dead, The Island, Statements after
an Arrest under the Immorality Act)

DIMETOS and TWO EARLY PLAYS
(Dimetos, No-Good Friday, Nongogo)

BOESMAN AND LENA and other plays
(The Blood Knot, People Are Living There, Hello and
Goodbye, Boesman and Lena)

A LESSON FROM ALOES

MASTER HAROLD . . . AND THE BOYS

THE ROAD TO MECCA

A Play in Two Acts

Suggested by the Life and Work
of Helen Martins of New Bethesda

ATHOL FUGARD

faber and faber
LONDON · BOSTON

First published in 1985
by Faber and Faber Limited
3 Queen Square London WC1N 3AU

Set by Wilmaset, Birkenhead
Printed in Great Britain by
Whitstable Litho Ltd., Whitstable, Kent

This play is fully protected by copyright and application
for public performance should be made to
William Morris Agency (UK) Ltd, 147/149 Wardour St, London W1V 3TB,
or to William Morris Agency, Inc., 1350 Avenue of the
Americas, New York, NY 10019, USA.

British Library Cataloguing in Publication Data

Fugard, Athol
The road to Mecca.
I. Title
822   PR9369.3.F8

ISBN 0-571-13691-5

For S.H.

The soul selects her own society –
Then – shuts the door –
On her divine majority –
Present no more.

Emily Dickinson

A NOTE ON MISS HELEN

Athol Fugard

It was a drive into the Karoo to spend a holiday on a friend's
farm and the route I drove that took me for the first time
through what had only been a name on a map until then: New
Bethesda, a small village in what turned out to be an absolutely
magnificent setting. As I drove through it, I couldn't help
responding to it, because I'm actually born in that part of the
world – as a matter of fact, I was born 15 miles away from New
Bethesda in a place called Middelburg. Driving to my friend's
farm I was struck by its isolation and thought to myself, hell,
this would be quite a nice place to have a house, and escape
from the city if ever I felt like getting away from the world. I
mentioned this to my friend who said, 'Well, you know, the
houses are dirt-cheap in New Bethesda because there has been a
move from the rural areas into the cities. You could pick up a
house there very cheaply.' So on the way back to Port Elizabeth,
I in fact stopped and inquired and looked around and discovered
there were houses for sale very, very cheaply.

I returned three months later with the express purpose of
buying a house, which I still own. In the course of looking at
various houses and getting to know a few of the locals, reference
was made to a rather strange character who lived in the village.
Her name was Helen Niemand and the people were kind of
apologetic about her because they regarded her as a little crazy.
They said that her craziness took the form of rather silly statues
and sculpture that she made and had all around her house. I
obviously couldn't resist the temptation of strolling in the
direction of her house and seeing Miss Helen's 'Mecca' for the
first time. She was still alive at that point but had become
virtually a total recluse. So, apart from seeing her in the distance
once or twice, and nodding at her when she was among her
statues and I happened to be walking past, I never got to know
her personally.

About two years after I bought my house and started visiting
the village regularly, Miss Helen committed suicide. Obviously,

About two years after I bought my house and started visiting the village regularly, Miss Helen committed suicide. Obviously, as a writer I couldn't help responding to this very eccentric character in this strange little community – a community which was in a sense hostile to her life and her work because it was a deviation from what they considered to be the way a life should be lived – and thinking: there's a damn good story. Over the next few years thoughts about Miss Helen occurred with some frequency in my notebooks.

I also began to discover more about the real Miss Helen. For example, up until the age of fifty, when her husband died, there was nothing about her that gave any hint of what was going to happen. Then her life suddenly erupted in this remarkable way in terms of her sculpture. Suddenly there was the first statue in the garden, and then over the next fifteen or seventeen years she worked away, with obsessive dedication, at what must have been a personal vision. After her death I went on to discover what she had done inside her house as well – as remarkable a feat as what she had done outside with the sculptures. Those seventeen years of creative activity ended, and there was a period of about eighteen months or two years during which she made nothing, did nothing and became very paranoid, very depressed. One night she killed herself by drinking caustic soda (the Americans would call it lye): she burned away her insides.

Though obviously in a sense provoked by Miss Helen's story, I've never quite been hooked by it. I'm a fisherman and I know the difference between a fish that's just playing with your bait and one that says, 'WRITE! I'M IT!' and takes your rod down and you sit back and put the hook deep in. I wasn't hooked.

The hooking came through a coincidence of factors. At a personal level, I began to realize, a provocation had been thrown at me four years previously by an actress who was doing *A Lesson from Aloes* in Amsterdam (she had also done *Boesman and Lena*). In the course of a conversation at the Rijksmuseum she said to me, 'Those are marvellous roles you have created for women. I'm very grateful to you for that, but, looking back at your work, I can't help being struck by the fact that you have never had two women together. When are you going to do that?'

And I suddenly registered for the first time that although I had created an interesting gallery of women's portraits over the years, I'd never put two women together on a stage as the focus of the whole event. Other personal factors in my life helped give the provocation more of an edge, more of a demand that I think about it, try to do something about it.

While this was happening to me, I discovered another fact about Miss Helen: that in the last years of her life, the last period of nothing until her death, there had been one very significant friendship – a friendship with a young woman, a social worker, from Cape Town. I'd rather not mention her name, because I've taken every liberty I felt necessary in writing the play. I've done my own thing; I've not written a documentary. I discovered that the friendship had been very, very meaningful. I accidentally happened to meet the young woman. I was struck by her because she was very strong, a very remarkable person, with a strong social conscience, a strong sense of what South Africa was about, a strong outrage at what was wrong with it. I couldn't help thinking of the anomaly of this sort of stern decency encountering the almost feudal world of New Bethesda – a South Africa which disappeared from the rest of the country a hundred years ago. Obviously, that young person had had quite a confrontation with the village.

Because of my respect for Miss Helen the young woman gave me, as a gesture, a little memento of the occasion when we met, a photograph of herself and Miss Helen. I took one look at the photograph – it's a brilliant, beautiful photograph – and there was the play. There was the coincidence. I was hooked. That was the moment when I swallowed the bait.

From an interview with Gitta Honegger, 1984
(first printed in Yale Reports)

CHARACTERS

MISS HELEN
ELSA
MARIUS BYLEVELD

The Road to Mecca opened at the Lyttelton Theatre, London, on 22 February 1985. The cast was as follows:

MISS HELEN	Yvonne Bryceland
ELSA	Charlotte Cornwell
MARIUS BYLEVELD	Bob Peck

Directed by	Athol Fugard
Designed by	Douglas Heap

The time: autumn 1974.

The lounge and, leading off it, the bedroom alcove of a house in the small Karoo village of New Bethesda. An extraordinary room by virtue of the attempt to use as much light and colour as is humanly possible. The walls—mirrors on all of them—are all of different colours, while on the ceiling and floor are solid, multi-coloured geometric patterns. Yet the final effect is not bizarre but rather one of light and extravagant fantasy. Just what the room is really about will be revealed later when its candles and lamps—again, a multitude of them of every size, shape and colour—are lit. The late afternoon light does, however, give some hint of the magic to come.

MISS HELEN is in the bedroom alcove. A frail, bird-like little woman in her late sixties. A suggestion of personal neglect, particularly in her clothes which are shabby and were put on with obvious indifference to the final effect. She is nervously fussing around an old-fashioned washstand, laying out towels, soap, etc., etc., and from time to time directs her attention to the lounge and a door leading from it to the rest of the house. In the course of moving around she sees an overnight bag and a briefcase on the floor near the lounge entrance. She fetches these and carries them into the alcove.

ELSA enters, a strong young woman in her late twenties dressed in a tracksuit or something else suitable for a long motorcar ride.

ELSA: Not cold enough yet for the car to freeze up, is it?
HELEN: No. No danger of that. We haven't had any frost yet.
ELSA: I'm too exhausted to put it away.
> (*Collapses on the bed.*)
> Whew! Thank God that's over. Another hour and I would have been wiped out. That road gets longer and longer every time.
HELEN: Your hot water is nearly ready.
ELSA: Good.
> (*Starts to unpack her overnight bag.*)
HELEN: Nice clean towels . . . and I've opened that box of

15

scented soaps you brought me last time.

ELSA: What? Oh, those. Haven't you used them yet?

HELEN: Of course not! I was keeping them for a special
occasion.

ELSA: And this is it?

HELEN: Yes. An unexpected visit from you is a *very* special
occasion. Is that all your luggage?

ELSA: When I said a short visit I really meant it.

HELEN: Such a long way to drive for just one night.

ELSA: I know.

HELEN: You don't think you could. . . ?

ELSA: Stay longer?

HELEN: Even just two nights?

ELSA: Impossible. We're right in the middle of exams. I've got
to be in that classroom at eight-thirty on Monday morning.
As it is I should be sitting at home right now marking
papers. I've even brought a pile of them with me just in
case I get a chance up here.
(*Starts to undress . . . tracksuit top, sneakers and socks.*)

HELEN: Put anything you want washed on one side and I'll get a
message to Katrina first thing in the morning.

ELSA: Don't bother her with that. I can do it myself.

HELEN: You can't leave without seeing Katrina! She'll never
forgive me if I don't let her know you're here. Please . . .
even if it's only for a few minutes.

ELSA: I won't leave without seeing Katrina, Miss Helen! But I
don't need her to wash a pair of pants and a bra for me. I
do my own washing.

HELEN: I'm sorry . . . I just thought you might . . . There's an
empty drawer here if you want to pack anything away.

ELSA: (*An edge to her voice*) Please stop fussing, Miss Helen! I
know my way around by now.

HELEN: It's just that if I'd known you were coming, I would
have had everything ready for you.

ELSA: Everything is fine just the way it is.

HELEN: No, it isn't! I don't even know that I've got enough in
the kitchen for a decent supper tonight. I did buy bread
yesterday, but for the rest . . .

16

ELSA: Please, Miss Helen! If we need anything, I'll get old
Retief to open his shop for us. In any case, I'm not hungry.
All I need at this moment is a good wash and a chance to
unwind so that I can forget I've been sitting in a motorcar
for twelve hours.

HELEN: Be patient with me, Elsie. Remember the little saying:
'Patience is a virtue, virtue is a grace, and . . .'

ELSA: (*Unexpectedly sharp*) For God's sake, Helen! Just leave me
alone for a few minutes!
(*Pause.*)

HELEN: (*Timidly*) I'll get your hot water.

(MISS HELEN *exits.* ELSA *slumps down on the bed, her head in
her hands.* MISS HELEN *returns a few seconds later with a
large kettle of hot water. She handles it with difficulty.*)
I've got the small one on for tea.

ELSA: Let me do that!

(*She jumps up and takes the kettle away from* MISS HELEN.
The two women stand staring at each other for a few seconds.
ELSA *puts down the kettle and then puts her hands on* MISS
HELEN's *shoulders.*)
My turn to say sorry.

HELEN: You don't need to do that.

ELSA: Please! It will help. Sorry, Miss Helen. I also need to hear
you say you forgive me.

HELEN: To tell you the truth, I was getting on my own nerves.

ELSA: (*Now smiling*) Come on.

HELEN: Oh, all right . . . But I promise you it isn't necessary.
You're forgiven.

ELSA: (*Leading* MISS HELEN *over to a chair*) Now sit down and
stop worrying about me. We're both going to close our
eyes, take a deep breath and start again. Ready?

HELEN: Ready.

ELSA: One, two, three . . .
(*Closed eyes and deep breaths.*)
And now?

HELEN: (*With the sly, tongue-in-cheek humour we will come to
recognize as characteristic of the relaxed* MISS HELEN) Well, if
you really mean it, I think the best thing is for you to get

17

back into your car, drive around the block and arrive again. And this time I want you, please, to hoot three times the way you usually do, so that I don't think a ghost has walked in through the front door when you appear.

ELSA: (*Calling Miss Helen's bluff*) Right. Where are the car keys?

(*Finds them and heads for the front door.*)

HELEN: Where are you going?

ELSA: To do what you said. Drive around the block and arrive again.

HELEN: Like that?

ELSA: Why, what's wrong?

HELEN: Elsie! Sterling Retief will have a heart attack if he sees you like that.

ELSA: But I wear less than this when I go to the beach. Oh, all right then, you old spoilsport, let's pretend.

(ELSA *runs into the other room, revs up her motorcar, grinds through all its gears and 'arrives'. Three blasts on the horn. The two women play the 'arrival game' [specifics to be determined in rehearsal]. At the end of it they come together in a good laugh.*)

If my friends in Cape Town were to have seen that! You must understand, Miss Helen, Elsa Barlow is known as a 'serious young woman'. Bit of a blue-stocking, in fact. Not much fun there! I don't know how you did it, Helen, but you caught me with those stockings down from the first day we met. You have the rare distinction of being the only person who can make me make a fool of myself . . . and enjoy it.

HELEN: You weren't making a fool of yourself. And anyway what about me? Nearly seventy and behaving as if I were seven!

ELSA: Let's face it, we've both still got a little girl hidden away in us somewhere.

HELEN: And they like to play together.

ELSA: Mine hasn't done that for a long time.

HELEN: And I didn't even know that mine was still alive.

ELSA: *That* she most certainly is. She's the one who comes running out to play first. Feeling better?

18

HELEN: Much better.

(*For the moment all tensions are gone.* ELSA *cleans herself as thoroughly as a basin of water, a face cloth and a bar of scented soap will allow.*)

ELSA: God, this Karoo dust gets right into your pores. I can even taste it. That first mouthful of tea is going to be mud. I'll fill up all the kettles tomorrow and have a really good scrub. When did you last have one?

(MISS HELEN *has to think about that.*)

Right, settled. Your name is down for one as well.

(*A few seconds of industrious scrubbing.* MISS HELEN *watches her.*)

What are you thinking?

HELEN: So many things! About the way you *did* arrive. I wasn't joking. For a few seconds I did think I was seeing a ghost. I heard the front door open . . . I thought it was little Katrina, she also never knocks . . . but instead there you were.

(*She wants to say more but stops herself.*)

ELSA: Go on.

HELEN: It was so strange. Almost as if you didn't really see me or anything else at first . . . didn't want to. And so cross! I've never seen you like that before.

ELSA: This isn't quite like the other times, Miss Helen.

HELEN: That's a pity. They were all good times.

(*Pause.*)

So what sort of time is this going to be? A bad one?

ELSA: (*Evenly*) I hope not. Doesn't have to be. It depends on you.

(MISS HELEN *avoids* ELSA'*s eyes. The young woman looks around the room.*)

But you're right. I hadn't really arrived until now.

HELEN: Where were you, Elsie?

ELSA: (*She thinks about the question before answering*) Way back at the turn-off to the village from the National Road . . . or maybe a few miles further along it now . . . walking to Cradock.

HELEN: I don't understand.

ELSA: I gave a lift to a woman outside Graaff-Reinet. That's most probably where she is now. I dropped her at the turn-off to the village.

HELEN: Who was she?

ELSA: (*Shrugging with apparent indifference*) An African woman.

HELEN: Cradock! That's a long walk.

ELSA: I know.

HELEN: It's about another eighty miles from the turn-off.
(*She waits for* ELSA *to say more.*)

ELSA: I nearly didn't stop for her. She didn't signal that she wanted a lift or anything like that. Didn't even look up when I passed . . . I was watching her in the rear-view mirror. Maybe that's what told me there was a long walk ahead of her . . . the way she had her head down and just kept on walking. And then the baby on her back. It was hot out there, Miss Helen, hot and dry and a lot of empty space . . . There wasn't a farmhouse in sight. She looked very small and unimportant in the middle of all that. Anyway, I stopped and reversed and offered her a lift. Not very graciously. I'd already been driving for ten hours and all I wanted was to get here as fast as I could. She got in and after a few miles we started talking. Her English wasn't very good, but when I finally got around to understanding what she was trying to tell me it added up to a good old South African story. Her husband, a farm labourer, had died recently, and no sooner had they buried him when the *Baas* told her to pack up and leave the farm. So there she was . . . on her way to the Cradock district, where she hoped to find a few distant relatives and a place to live.
(*Trying to remember the woman as clearly as possible.*)
About my age. The baby couldn't have been more than a few months old. All she had with her was one of those plastic shopping bags they put your groceries in at supermarkets. I saw a pair of old slippers. She was barefoot.

HELEN: Poor woman.

ELSA: So I dropped her at the turn-off. Gave her what was left of my food and some money. She carried on walking

20

and I drove here.

(*Pause.*)

HELEN: Is there something else?

ELSA: No. That's all.

HELEN: I'm sure somebody else will give her a lift.

ELSA: (*Too easily*) Hope so. If not, she and her baby are in for a night beside the road. There's eighty miles of the Karoo ahead of her. Shadows were already stretching out across the veld when she got out of the car. The Great Karoo! And just when I thought I was getting used to it, beginning to like it, in fact. Down in Cape Town I've actually caught myself talking rubbish about its vast space and emptiness, its awesome stillness and silence! Just like old Getruida down the road. It's that all right, but only because everything else has been all but damned out of existence. It's so obvious where you Afrikaners get your ideas of God from. Beats me how you've put up with it so long, Miss Helen. Nearly seventy years? My God, you deserve a medal. I would have packed up and left it at the first opportunity . . . and let's face it, you've had plenty of those.

HELEN: I was born here, Elsa.

ELSA: I sympathize, Miss Helen. Believe me, I truly sympathize.

HELEN: It's not really as bad as you make it sound. The few times I've been away, I've always ended up missing it and longing to be back.

ELSA: Because you wanted to get back to your work.

HELEN: (*Shaking her head*) No. Even before all that started. It grows on you, Elsa.

ELSA: Which is just about the only growing it seems to allow. For the rest, it's as merciless as the religion they preach around here. Looking out of the car window this afternoon I think I finally understood a few things about you Afrikaners . . . and it left me feeling just a little uneasy.

HELEN: You include me in all you're saying.

ELSA: Yes. You might not go to church any more, but you're still an Afrikaner, Miss Helen. You were in there with

them, singing hymns every Sunday, for a long, long time.
Bit of a renegade now, I admit, but you're still one at heart.

HELEN: And that heart is merciless?

(*Pause.*)

ELSA: No. That you aren't. A lot of other things maybe, but
certainly not that. Sorry, sorry, sorry . . .

HELEN: You're still very cross, aren't you? And something else
as well. There's a new sound in your voice. One I haven't
heard before.

ELSA: What do you mean?

HELEN: Like the way you talked about that woman on the road.
Almost as if you didn't care, which I know isn't true.

ELSA: Of course I cared. I cared enough to stop and pick her
up, to give her money and food. But I also don't want to
fool myself. That was a sop to my conscience and nothing
more. It wasn't a real contribution to her life and what she
is up against. Anyway, what's the point in talking about
her? She's most probably curling up in a stormwater drain
at this moment – that's where she said she'd sleep if she
didn't get a lift – and I feel better for a good wash.

HELEN: There it is again.

ELSA: Well, it's the truth.

HELEN: It was the way you said it.

ELSA: You're imagining things, Miss Helen. Come on, let's talk
about something else. It's too soon to get serious. We've got
enough time, and reasons, for that later on. What's been
happening in the village? Give me the news. Your last letter
didn't have much of that in it.

(ELSA *gets into clean clothes.* MISS HELEN *starts to fold the
discarded tracksuit.* ELSA *stops her.*)

I can do that.

HELEN: I just wanted to help.

ELSA: And you can do that by making a nice pot of tea and
giving me the village gossip.

(MISS HELEN *goes into the lounge. She takes cups and saucers,
etc., from a sideboard and places them on the table.*)

HELEN: I haven't got any gossip. Little Katrina is the only one
who really visits me any more, and all she wants to talk

about these days is her baby. There's also Marius, of course, but he never gossips.

ELSA: He still comes snooping around, does he?

HELEN: Don't put it like that, Elsa. He's a very old friend.

ELSA: Good luck to him. I hope the friendship continues. It's just that *I* wouldn't want him for one. Sorry, Miss Helen, but I don't trust your old friend, and I have a strong feeling that Pastor Marius Byleveld feels the same way about me. So let's change the subject. Tell me about Katrina. What has she been up to?

HELEN: She's fine. And so is the baby. As prettily dressed these days as any white baby, thanks to the clothes you sent her. She's been very good to me, Elsa. Never passes my front door without dropping in for a little chat. Is always asking about you. I don't know what I would do without her. But I'm afraid Koos has started drinking again. And making all sorts of terrible threats about her and the baby. He still doesn't believe it's his child.

ELSA: Is he beating her?

HELEN: No. The warning you gave him last time seems to have put a stop to that.

ELSA: God, it makes me sick! Why doesn't she leave him?

HELEN: And then do what?

ELSA: Find somebody else! Somebody who will value her as a human being and take care of her and the child.

HELEN: She can't do that, Elsie. They're married.

ELSA: Oh, for God's sake, Helen. There's the Afrikaner in you speaking. There is nothing sacred about a marriage that abuses the woman! I'll have a talk to her tomorrow. Let's make sure we get a message to her to come around.

HELEN: Don't make things more difficult for her, Elsa.

ELSA: How much more difficult can 'things' be than being married to a drunken bully? She *has* got a few rights, Miss Helen, and I just want to make sure she knows what they are. How old is she now?

HELEN: Seventeen, I think.

ELSA: At that age I was still at school dreaming about my future, and here she is with a baby and bruises. Quick, tell

23

me something else.

HELEN: Let me see . . . Good gracious me! Of course, yes! I have got important news. Old Getruida has got the whole village up in arms. Brace yourself, Elsa. She's applied for a licence to open a liquor store.

ELSA: A what?

HELEN: A liquor store. Alcoholic beverages.

ELSA: Booze in New Bethesda?

HELEN: If you want to put it that bluntly . . . yes.

ELSA: Now that *is* headline material. Good for old Gerty. I always knew she liked her sundowner, but I never thought she'd have the spunk to go that far.

HELEN: Don't joke about it, Elsie. It's a very serious matter. The village is very upset.

ELSA: Headed, no doubt, by your old friend Pastor Marius Byleveld.

HELEN: That's right. I understand that his last sermon was all about the evils of alcohol and how it's ruining the health and lives of our Coloured folk. Getruida says he's taking unfair advantage of the pulpit and that the Coloureds get it anyway from Graaff-Reinet.

ELSA: Then tell her to demand a turn.

HELEN: At what?

ELSA: The pulpit. Tell her to demand her right to get up there and put her case . . . and remind her before she does that the first miracle was water into wine.

HELEN: (*Trying not to laugh*) You're terrible, Elsie! Old Getruida in the pulpit!

ELSA: And you're an old hypocrite, Miss Helen. You love it when I make fun of the Church.

HELEN: No, I don't. I was laughing at Gerty, not the Church. And you have no right to make me laugh. It's a very serious matter.

ELSA: Of course it is! Which is why I want to know who you think is worse: the Dominee deciding what is right and wrong for the Coloured folk or old Getruida exploiting their misery?

HELEN: I'm afraid it's even more complicated than that, Elsa.

Marius *is* only thinking about what's best for them, but on the other hand Getruida has offered to donate part of her profits to their school building fund. And what about Koos? Wouldn't it make things even worse for Katrina if he had a local supply?

ELSA: They are two separate issues, Miss Helen. You don't punish a whole community because one man can't control his drinking. Which raises yet another point: has anybody bothered to ask the Coloured people what they think about it all?

HELEN: Are we going to have that argument again?

ELSA: I'm not trying to start an argument. But it does seem to me right and proper that if you're going to make decisions which affect other people, you should find out what those people think.

HELEN: It is the same argument. You know they don't do that here.

ELSA: Well, it's about time they started. I don't make decisions affecting the pupils at school without giving them a chance to say something. And they're children! We're talking about adult men and women in the year 1974.

HELEN: Those attitudes might be all right in Cape Town, Elsa, but you should know by now that the Valley has got its own way of doing things.

ELSA: Well, it can't cut itself off from the twentieth century for ever. Honestly, coming here is like stepping into the middle of a Chekhov play. While the rest of the world is hoping the bomb won't drop today, you people are arguing about who owns the Cherry Orchard. Your little world is not as safe as you would like to believe, Helen. If you think it's going to be left alone to stagnate in the nineteenth century while the rest of us hold our breath hoping we'll reach the end of the twentieth, you're in for one hell of a surprise. And it will start with your Coloured folk. They're not fools. They also read newspapers, you know. And if you don't believe me, try talking about something other than the weather and her baby next time Katrina comes around. You'll be surprised at what's going on inside that little head. As for you Helen!

Sometimes the contradictions in you make me want to scream. Why do you always stand up and defend this bunch of bigots? Look at the way they've treated you.

HELEN: (*Getting nervous*) They leave me alone now.

ELSA: That is not what you said in your last letter!

HELEN: My last letter?

ELSA: Yes.

(*Pause.* HELEN *has tensed.*)

Are you saying you don't remember it, Helen?

HELEN: No . . . I remember it.

ELSA: And what you said in it?

HELEN: (*Trying to escape*) Please, little Elsie! Not now. Let's talk about it later. I'm still all flustered with you arriving so unexpectedly. Give me a chance to collect my wits together. Please? And while I'm doing that, I'll make that pot of tea you asked for.

(MISS HELEN *exits into the kitchen.* ELSA *takes stock of the room. Not an idle examination; rather, she is trying to see it objectively, trying to understand something . . . She spends a few seconds at the window, staring out at the statues in the yard. She sees a cardboard box in a corner and opens it— handfuls of coloured ceramic chips. She also discovers a not very successful attempt to hide an ugly burn mark on one of the walls.* MISS HELEN *returns with tea and biscuits.*)

ELSA: What happened here?

HELEN: Oh, don't worry about that. I'll get Koos or somebody to put a coat of paint over it.

ELSA: But what happened?

HELEN: One of the lamps started smoking badly when I was out of the room.

ELSA: And new curtains.

HELEN: Yes. I got tired of the old ones. I found a few Marie biscuits in the pantry. Will you be mother?

(*Light is starting to fade in the room.* ELSA *pours the tea, dividing her attention between that and studying the older woman.* MISS HELEN *tries to hide her unease.*)

Do I get a turn now to ask for news?

ELSA: No.

26

HELEN: Why not?

ELSA: I haven't come up here to talk about myself.

HELEN: That's not fair!

ELSA: It's boring.

HELEN: Not to me. Come on Elsie, fair is fair. You asked me for the village gossip and I did my best. Now it's your turn.

ELSA: What do you want to know?

HELEN: Everything you would have told me about in your letters if you had kept your promise and written them.

ELSA: Good and bad news?

HELEN: I said everything . . . but try to make the good a little bit more than the bad.

ELSA: Right. The *Elsa Barlow Advertiser*! Hot off the presses! What do you want to start with? Financial, crime or sports page?

HELEN: The front-page headline.

ELSA: How's this? 'Barlow to appear before School Board for possible disciplinary action.'

HELEN: Not again!

ELSA: Yep.

HELEN: Oh dear! What was it this time?

ELSA: Wait for the story. 'Elsa Barlow, a twenty-eight-year-old English language teacher, is to appear before a Board of Enquiry of the Cape Town School Board. She faces the possibility of strict disciplinary action. The enquiry follows a number of complaints from the parents of pupils in Miss Barlow's Standard Nine class. It is alleged that in April this year Miss Barlow asked the class, as a homework exercise, to write a five-hundred word letter to the State President on the subject of racial inequality. Miss Barlow teaches at a Coloured School.'

HELEN: Is that true?

ELSA: Are you doubting the accuracy and veracity of the *Advertiser*?

HELEN: Elsie! Elsie! Sometimes I think you deliberately look for trouble.

ELSA: All I 'deliberately look for', Miss Helen, are opportunities

27

to make those young people in my classroom think for
themselves.

HELEN: So what is going to happen?

ELSA: Depends on me, I suppose. If I appear before them
contrite and apologetic, a stern reprimand. But if I behave
the way I really feel, I suppose I could lose my job.

HELEN: Do you want my advice?

ELSA: No.

HELEN: Well, I'm going to give it to you all the same. Say
you're sorry and that you won't do it again.

ELSA: Both of those are lies, Miss Helen.

HELEN: Only little white ones.

ELSA: God, I'd give anything to be able to walk in and tell that
School Board exactly what I think of them and their
educational system. But you're right, there are the pupils as
well, and for as long as I'm in the classroom a little
subversion is possible. Rebellion starts, Miss Helen, with
just one man or woman standing up and saying, 'No.
Enough!' Albert Camus. French writer.

HELEN: You make me nervous when you talk like that.

ELSA: And you sound just like one of those parents. You know
something? I think you're history's first reactionary-
revolutionary. You're a double agent, Helen!

HELEN: Haven't you got any good news?

ELSA: Lots. I still don't smoke. I drink very moderately. I try to
jog a few miles every morning.

HELEN: You're not saying anything about David.

ELSA: Turn to the lonely hearts column. There's a sad little
paragraph: 'Young lady seeks friendship with young man,
etc., etc.'

HELEN: You're talking in riddles. I was asking you about David.

ELSA: And I'm answering you. I've said nothing about him
because there's nothing to say. It's over.

HELEN: You mean . . . you and David . . . ?

ELSA: Yes, that is exactly what I mean. It's finished. We don't
see each other any more.

HELEN: I knew there was something wrong from the moment
you walked in.

ELSA: If you think this is me with something wrong, you should have been around two months ago. Your little Elsie was in a bad way. You were in line for an unexpected visit a lot earlier than this, Helen.

HELEN: You should have come.

ELSA: I nearly did. But your letters suggested that you weren't having such a good time either. If we'd got together at that point, we might have come up with a suicide pact.

HELEN: I don't think so.

ELSA: Joke, Miss Helen.

HELEN: Then don't joke about those things. Weren't you going to tell me?

ELSA: I'm trying to forget it, Helen! There's another reason why I didn't come up. It has left me with a profound sense of shame.

HELEN: Of what?

ELSA: Myself. The whole stupid mess.

HELEN: Mess?

ELSA: Yes, mess! Have you got a better word to describe a situation so rotten with lies and deceit that your only sense of yourself is one of disgust?

HELEN: And you were so happy when you told me about him on your last visit.

ELSA: God, that was more than just happiness, Miss Helen. It was like discovering the reason for being the person, the woman, I am for the first time in my life. And a little bit scary . . . realizing that another person could do so much to your life, to your sense of yourself. Even before it all went wrong, there were a couple of times when I wasn't so sure I liked it.

HELEN: But what happened? Was there a row about something?

ELSA: (*Bitter little laugh*) Row? Oh, Helen! Yes, there were plenty of those. But they were incidental. There had to be some sort of noise, so we shouted at each other. We also cried. We did everything you're supposed to.

HELEN: All I know about him is what you told me. He sounded like such a sensitive and good man, well-read and intelligent. So right for you.

29

ELSA: He was all of that.
> (*A moment's hesitation. She is not certain about saying something. She decides to take the chance.*)
> There's also something about him I didn't tell you. He's married. He has a devoted, loving wife – quite pretty in fact – and a child. A little girl. Shocked you?

HELEN: Yes. You should have told me, Elsie. I would have warned you.

ELSA: That's exactly why I didn't. I knew you would, but I was going to prove you wrong. Anyway, I didn't need any warnings. Anything you could have said to me, Helen, I'd said to myself from the very beginning . . . but I was going to prove myself wrong as well. What it all came down to finally was that there were two very different ideas about what was happening, and we discovered it too late. You see, I was in it for keeps, Helen. I knew that we were all going to get hurt, that somehow we would all end up being victims of the situation . . . but I also believed that when the time came to choose I would be the lucky winner, that he would leave his wife and child and go with me. Boy, was I wrong! Ding-dong, wrong-wrong, tolls Elsa's bell at the close of the day!

HELEN: Don't do that.

ELSA: Defence mechanism. It still hurts. I'm getting impatient for the time when I'll be able to laugh at it all. I mustn't make him sound like a complete bastard. He wasn't without a conscience. Far from it. If anything, it was too big. The end would have been a lot less messy if he'd known how to just walk away and close the door behind him. When finally the time for that did come, he sat around in pain and torment, crying – God, that was awful! – waiting for me to tell him to go back to his wife and child. Should have seen him, Helen. He came up with postures of despair that would have made Michelangelo jealous. I know it's all wrong to find another person's pain disgusting, but that is what eventually happened. The last time he crucified himself on the sofa in my lounge I felt like vomiting. He told me just once too often how much he hated himself for hurting me.

HELEN: Elsie, my poor darling. Come here.

ELSA: (*Taut*) I'm all right now.

(*Pause.*)

Do you know what the really big word is, Helen? I had it all wrong. Like most people, I suppose I used to think it was 'love'. That's the big one all right, and it's quite an event when it comes along. But there's an even bigger one. Trust. And more dangerous. Because that's when you drop your defences, lay yourself wide open, and if you've made a mistake, you're in big, big trouble. And it hurts like hell. Ever heard the story about the father giving his son his first lesson in business?

(MISS HELEN *shakes her head.*)

I think it's meant to be a joke, so remember to laugh. He puts his little boy high up on something or other and says to him, 'Jump. Don't worry, I'll catch you.' The child is nervous, of course, but Daddy keeps reassuring him: 'I'll catch you.' Eventually the little boy works up enough courage and does jump, and Daddy, of course, doesn't make a move to catch him. When the child has stopped crying – because he has hurt himself – the father says: 'Your first lesson in business, my son. Don't trust anybody.'

(*Pause.*)

If you tell it with a Jewish accent, it's even funnier.

HELEN: I don't think it's funny.

ELSA: I think it's ugly. That little boy is going to think twice about jumping again, and at this moment the same goes for Elsa Barlow.

HELEN: Don't speak too soon, Elsie. Life has surprised me once or twice.

ELSA: I'm talking about trust, Miss Helen. I can see myself loving somebody else again. Not all that interested in it right at the moment, but there's an even chance that it will happen again. Doesn't seem as if we've got much choice in the matter anyway. But trusting?

HELEN: You can have the one without the other?

ELSA: Oh yes. That much I've learned. I went on loving David

long after I realized I couldn't trust him any more. That is
why life is just a bit complicated at the moment. A little of
that love is still hanging around.

HELEN: I've never really thought about it.

ELSA: Neither had I. It needs a betrayal to get you going.

HELEN: Then I suppose I've been lucky. I never had any
important trusts to betray . . . until I met you. My
marriage might have looked like that, but it was habit that
kept Stefanus and me together. I was never . . . open? . . .
to him. Was that the phrase you used?

ELSA: Wide open.

HELEN: That's it! It's a good one. I was never 'wide open' to
anyone. But with you all of that changed. So it's as simple
as that. Trust. I've always tried to understand what made
you, and being with you, so different from anything else in
my life. But, of course, that's it. I trust you. That's why my
little girl can come out and play. All the doors are wide
open!

ELSA: (*Breaking the mood*) So there, Miss Helen. You asked for
the news . . .

HELEN: I almost wish I hadn't.
(*Light has now faded.* MISS HELEN *fetches a box of matches
and lights the candles on the table. The room floats up gently
out of the gloom, the mirrors and glitter on the walls reflecting
the candle light.* ELSA *picks up one of the candles and walks
around the room with it, and we see something of the magic to
come.*)

ELSA: Still works, Miss Helen. In the car driving up I was
wondering if the novelty would have worn off a little. But
here it is again. You're a little wizard, you know. You make
magic with your mirrors and glitter. 'Never light a candle
carelessly, and be sure you know what you're doing when
you blow one out!' Remember saying that?

HELEN: To myself, yes. Many times.

ELSA: And to me . . . after you had stopped laughing at the
expression on my face when you lit them for the first time.
'Light is a miracle, Miss Barlow, which even the most
ordinary human being can make happen.' We had just had

our first pot of tea together. Maybe I do take it all just a little for granted now. But that first time . . . I wish I could make you realize what it's like to be walking down a dusty, deserted little street in a God-forsaken village in the middle of the Karoo, bored to death by the heat and flies and silence, and then to be stopped in your tracks – and I mean stopped! – by all of that out there. And then, having barely recovered from that, to come inside and find *this*! Believe me Helen, when I saw your 'Mecca' for the first time, I just stood there and gaped. 'What in God's name am I looking at? Camels and pyramids? Not three, but dozens of Wise Men? Owls with old motorcar headlights for eyes? Peacocks with more colour and glitter than the real birds? Heat stroke? Am I hallucinating?' And then you! Standing next to a mosque made out of beer bottles and staring back at me like one of your owls!

(*A good laugh at the memory.*)

She's mad. No question about it. Everything they've told me about her is true. A genuine Karoo nutcase.

(*Walking carefully around* MISS HELEN *in a mock attitude of wary and suspicious examination.*)

Doesn't look dangerous, though. Wait . . . she's smiling! Be careful, Barlow! Could be a trick. They didn't say she was violent, though. Just mad. Mad as a hatter. Go on. Take a chance. Say hello and see what happens. 'Hello!'

(*Both women laugh.*)

HELEN: You're exaggerating. It wasn't like that at all.

ELSA: Yes, it was.

HELEN: And I'm saying it wasn't. To start with, it wasn't the mosque. I was repairing a mermaid.

ELSA: I forgot the mermaids!

HELEN: (*Serenely certain*) And I was the one who spoke first. I asked you to point out the direction to Mecca. You made a mistake, and so I corrected you. Then I invited you into the yard, showed you around, after which we came into the house for that pot of tea.

ELSA: That is precisely what I mean! Who would ever believe it? That you found yourself being asked to point out the

33

direction to Mecca – not London, or New York, or Paris, but Mecca – in the middle of the Karoo by a little lady no bigger than a bird, surrounded by camels and owls . . . and mermaids! . . . made of cement? Who in their right mind is going to believe that? And then this (*the room*), your little miracle of light and colour.

(MISS HELEN *is smiling with suppressed pride and pleasure.*) You were proud of yourself, weren't you? Come on, admit it.

HELEN: (*Trying hard to contain her emotion*) Yes, I admit I was a little proud.

ELSA: Miss Helen, just a little?

HELEN: (*She can't hold back any longer*) All right, then, no! Not just a little. Oh, most definitely not. I was prouder of myself that day than I had ever been in my life. Nobody before you, or since, has done that to me. I was tingling all over with excitement as we walked around the yard looking at the statues. All those years of working on my Mecca had at last been vindicated. I've got a silly little confession to make about that first meeting. When we came inside and were sitting in here talking and drinking tea and the light started to fade and it became time to light a candle . . . I suddenly realized I was beginning to feel shy, more shy than I had even been with Stefanus on my wedding night. It got so bad I was half-wishing you would stand up and say it was time to go! You see, when I lit the candles you were finally going to see all of me. I don't mean my face, or the clothes I was wearing – you had already seen all of that out in the yard – I mean the *real* me, because that is what this room is . . . and I desperately, oh so desperately, wanted you to like what you saw. By the time we met I had got used to rude eyes staring at me and my work, dismissing both of them as ugly. I'd lived with those eyes for fifteen years, and they didn't bother me any more. Yours were different. In just the little time we had already been together I had ended up feeling . . . No, more than that: I *knew* I could trust them. There's our big word again, Elsie! I was so nervous I didn't know what we were talking about any more while I sat here trying to find enough courage to

34

get a box of matches and light the candles. But eventually I did and you . . . you looked around the room and laughed with delight! You liked what you saw! This is the best of me, Elsa. This is what I really am. Forget everything else. Nothing, not even my name or my face, is me as much as those Wise Men and their camels travelling to the East, or the light and glitter in this room. The mermaids, the wise old owls, the gorgeous peacocks . . . all of them are *me*. And I had delighted you!

Dear God. If you only knew what you did for my life that day. How much courage, how much faith in it you gave me. Because all those years of being laughed at and thought a mad old woman had taken their toll, Elsie. When you walked into my life that afternoon I hadn't been able to work or make anything for nearly a year . . . and I was beginning to think I wouldn't ever again, that I had reached the end. The only reason I've got for being alive is my Mecca. Without that I'm . . . nothing . . . a useless old woman getting on everybody's nerves . . . and that is exactly what I had started to feel like. You revived my life.

I didn't sleep that night after you left. My Mecca was a long way from being finished! All the things I still had to do, all the statues I still had to make, came crowding in on me when I went to bed. I thought my head was going to burst! I've never been so impatient with darkness all my life. I sat up in bed all night waiting for the dawn to come so that I could start working again, and then just go on working and working.

ELSA: And you certainly did that, Miss Helen. On my next trip you proudly introduced me to a very stern Buddha, remember? The cement was still wet.

HELEN: That's quite right. That was my next one.

ELSA: Then came the Easter Island head, the one with the topknot.

HELEN: Correct.

ELSA: And you still haven't explained to me what it's doing in Mecca – and, for that matter, wise old owls and mermaids as well.

HELEN: My Mecca has got a logic of its own, Elsa. Even I don't properly understand it.

ELSA: And then my favourite! That strange creature, half-cock, half-man, on the point of dropping his trousers. Really Helen!

HELEN: That one is pure imagination. I don't know where it comes from. And I've told you before, he's not dropping his trousers, he's pulling them up.

ELSA: And I remain unconvinced. Take another good look at the expression on his face. That's anticipation, not satisfaction. Any surprises this time?

(*Pause.*)

HELEN: This time?

ELSA: Yes.

HELEN: No. There aren't any surprises this time.

ELSA: Work in progress?

HELEN: Not at the moment. I haven't managed to get started on anything since you were last here.

ELSA: What happened to the moon-mosaic? Remember? Against the back wall! You were going to use those ceramic chips I brought you.

HELEN: They're safe. There in the corner.

ELSA: Yes, I saw them . . . in exactly the same spot where I left them three months ago. It sounded such a wonderful idea, Helen. You were so excited when you told me about it.

HELEN: And I still am. I've still got it.

ELSA: So what are you waiting for? Roll up your sleeves and get on with it.

HELEN: It's not as simple as that, Elsie. You see . . . that's the trouble. It's still only just an *idea* I'm *thinking* about. I can't see it clearly enough yet to start work on it. I've told you before, Elsie, I have to *see* them very clearly first. They've got to come to me inside like pictures. And if they don't, well, all I can do is wait . . . and hope that they will. I wish I knew how to make it happen, but I don't. I don't know where the pictures come from. I can't force myself to see something that isn't there. I've tried to do that once or

36

twice in the past when I was desperate, but the work always ended up a lifeless, shapeless mess. If they don't come, all I can do is wait . . . which is what I'm doing.

(MISS HELEN *is revealing a lot of inner agitation.*)

ELSA: (*Carefully*) I'm listening, Miss Helen. Go on.

HELEN: I try to be patient with myself, but it's hard. There isn't all that much time left . . . and then my eyes . . . and my hands . . . they're not what they used to be. But the worst thing of all is . . . suppose that I'm waiting for nothing, that there won't be any more pictures inside ever again, that this time I *have* reached the end? Oh God, no! Please no. Anything but that. You do understand, don't you, Elsie?

ELSA: I think I do.

(*She speaks quietly. It is not going to be easy.*)

Come and sit down here with me, Helen.

(MISS HELEN *does so, but apprehensively.*)

It's time to talk about your last letter, Helen.

HELEN: Do we have to do that now? Can't it wait?

ELSA: No.

HELEN: Please.

ELSA: Sorry, Helen, but we've only got tonight.

HELEN: Then don't spoil it!

ELSA: Helen . . . that letter is the reason for me being here. You do realize that, don't you?

HELEN: Yes. I guessed that was the reason for your visit. But you must make allowances, little Elsie. I wasn't feeling very well when I wrote it.

ELSA: That much is obvious.

HELEN: But I've cheered up ever so much since then. Truly. And now with your visit . . . I just know everything is going to be all right again. I was very depressed you see. I wrote it in a bad depression. But I regretted posting it the moment after I had dropped it into the letter box. I even thought about asking the Postmaster if I could have it back.

ELSA: Why didn't you?

(*Pause.*)

Or send me a telegram: 'Ignore last letter. Feeling much better.' Six words. That would have done it.

37

HELEN: I didn't think of that.

ELSA: We're wasting precious time. You wrote it, posted it, and I received it.

HELEN: So can't we now, please, just forget it?

ELSA: (*Disbelief*) Miss Helen, do you remember what you said in it?

HELEN: Vaguely.

ELSA: That's not good enough.

(*She goes to the bedroom alcove and fetches the letter from her briefcase.*)

HELEN: What are you going to do?

ELSA: Read it.

HELEN: No! I don't want to hear it.

ELSA: You already have, Miss Helen. You wrote it.

HELEN: But I don't want to talk about it.

ELSA: Yes, you must.

HELEN: Don't bully me, Elsa! You know I don't know how to fight back. Please . . . not tonight. Can't we . . . ?

ELSA: No, we can't. For God's sake, Helen! We've only got tonight and maybe a little of tomorrow to talk.

HELEN: But you mustn't take it seriously.

ELSA: Too late, Helen. I already have. I've driven eight hundred miles without a break because of this. And don't lie to me. You meant every word of it.

(*Pause.*)

I'm not trying to punish you for writing it. I've come because I want to try and help.

(ELSA *sits down at the table, pulls the candle closer and reads. She struggles a little to decipher words. The handwriting is obviously bad.*)

'My very own and dearest little Elsie,

Have you finally also deserted me? This is my fourth letter to you and still no reply. Have I done something wrong? This must surely be the darkest night of my soul. I thought I had lived through that fifteen years ago, but I was wrong. This is worse. Infinitely worse. I had nothing to lose that night. Nothing in my life was precious or worth holding on to. Now there is so much and I am losing it all . . . you, the house, my work, my Mecca. I can't fight them alone, little Elsie. I need you. Don't you care about me any more? It is only through your eyes that I now see my Mecca. I need you, Elsie. My eyesight is so bad that I can barely see the words I am writing. And my hands can hardly hold the pen. Help me, little Elsie. Everything is ending and I am alone in the dark. There is no light left. I would rather do away with myself than carry on like this.

   Your ever-loving and anguished
      Helen.'
(ELSA *carefully folds up the letter and puts it back in the envelope.*)
What's all that about losing your house. Who's trying to get you out?

HELEN: I exaggerated a little. They're not really being nasty about it.

ELSA: Who?

HELEN: The Church Council. They say it's for my own good. And I do understand what they mean, it's just that . . .

ELSA: Slowly, Miss Helen, slowly. I still don't know what you're talking about. Start from the beginning. What has the Church Council got to do with you and the house? I thought it was yours.

HELEN: It is.

ELSA: So?

HELEN: It's not the house, Elsa. It's me. They discussed me . . . my situation . . . at one of their meetings.

ELSA: (*Disbelief and anger*) They *what*?

HELEN: That's how Marius put it. He . . . he said they were worried about me living here alone.

ELSA: *They* are worried about *you*?

HELEN: Yes. It's my health they are worried about.

ELSA: (*Shaking her head*) When it comes to hypocrisy – and blatant hypocrisy at that – you Afrikaners are in a class by yourselves. So tell me, did they also discuss Getruida's situation? And what about Mrs van Heerden down at the other end of the village? They're about the same age as you and they also live alone.

39

HELEN: That's what I said. But Marius said it's different with them.

ELSA: In what way?

HELEN: Well, you see, because of my hands and everything else, they don't believe I can look after myself so well any more.

ELSA: Are they right?

HELEN: No! I'm quite capable of looking after myself.

ELSA: And where are you supposed to go if you leave the village? To a niece, four times removed, in Durban, whom you've only seen a couple of times in your life?

(MISS HELEN *goes to a little table at the back and fetches a form which she hands to* ELSA.)

(*Reading*) 'Sunshine Home for the Aged'. I see. So it's like that, is it? That's the lovely old house on the left when you come into Graaff-Reinet, next to the church. In fact, it's run by the church, isn't it?

HELEN: Yes.

ELSA: That figures. It's got a beautiful garden, Miss Helen. Whenever I drive past on my way up here there are always a few old folk in their 'twilight years' sitting around enjoying the sunshine. It's well named. It all looks very restful. So that's what they want to do with you. This is not your handwriting.

HELEN: No. Marius filled it in for me.

ELSA: Very considerate of him.

HELEN: He's coming to fetch it tonight.

ELSA: For an old friend he sounds a little over-eager to have you on your way, Miss Helen.

HELEN: It's just that they've got a vacancy at the moment. They're usually completely full. There's a long waiting list. But I haven't signed it yet!

(ELSA *studies* MISS HELEN *in silence for a few moments*.)

ELSA: How bad are your hands? Be honest with me.

HELEN: They're not *that* bad. I exaggerated a little in my letter.

ELSA: You could still work with them if you wanted to?

HELEN: Yes.

ELSA: Is there anything you can't do?

40

HELEN: I can do anything I want to, Elsie . . . if I make the effort.

ELSA: Let me see them.

HELEN: Please don't. I'm ashamed of them.

ELSA: Come on.

(MISS HELEN *holds out her hands.* ELSA *examines them.*)
And these scabs?

HELEN: They're nothing. A little accident at the stove. I was making prickly-pear syrup for you.

ELSA: There seem to have been a lot of little accidents lately. Better be more careful.

HELEN: I will. I definitely will.

ELSA: Pain?

HELEN: Just a little.

(*While* ELSA *studies her hands:*)
Just that one letter after your last visit, saying you had arrived back safely and would be writing again soon, and then nothing. Three months.

ELSA: I did write, Helen. Two very long letters.

HELEN: I never got them.

ELSA: Because I never posted them.

HELEN: Elsie! Why? They would have made all the difference in the world.

ELSA: (*Shaking her head*) No. Muddled, confused, full of self-pity. Knowing now what you were trying to deal with here, they were hardly what you needed in your life.

HELEN: You're very wrong. Anything would have been better than nothing.

ELSA: No, Helen. Believe me nothing was better than those two letters. I've still got them at home. I read them now whenever I need to count my blessings. They remind me of the mess I was in.

HELEN: That's why I feel so bad now about the letter I wrote you. My problems seem so insignificant compared with yours.

ELSA: Don't let's start that, Helen. Sorting our problem priorities isn't going to get us anywhere. In any case, mine are over and done with . . . which leaves us with you. So what are you going to do?

(MISS HELEN *doesn't answer.* ELSA *is beginning to lose patience.*)

Come *on*, Helen! If I hadn't turned up tonight, what were you going to say to Dominee Marius Byleveld when he came around?

HELEN: I was going to ask him to give me a little more time to think about it.

ELSA: You were going to *ask* him for it, not *tell* him you *wanted* it? And *do* you need more time to think about it? I thought you knew what you wanted?

HELEN: Of course I do.

ELSA: Then tell me again. And say it simply. I need to hear it.

HELEN: You know I can't leave here, Elsa!

ELSA: For a moment I wasn't so sure. So then what's the problem? When he comes around tonight hand this back to him . . . unsigned . . . and say no. Thank him for his trouble but tell him you are perfectly happy where you are and quite capable of looking after yourself.

(MISS HELEN *hesitates. A sense of increasing emotional confusion and uncertainty.*)

Helen, you have just said that is what you want.

HELEN: I know. It's just that Marius is such a persuasive talker.

ELSA: Then talk back!

HELEN: I'm not very good at that. Won't you help me, little Elsie, please, and speak to him as well? You are so much better at arguing than me.

ELSA: No, I won't! And for God's sake stop behaving like a naughty child who's been called to the principal's office. I'm sorry, but the more I hear about your Marius, the worse it gets. If you want my advice, you'll keep the two of us well away from each other. I *won't* argue with him on your behalf because there is nothing to argue about. This is not his house, and it most certainly is not his life that is being discussed at Church Council meetings. Who the hell do they think they are? Sitting around a table deciding what is going to happen to you!

HELEN: Marius did say that they were trying to think of what

42

was best for me.

ELSA: No, they're not! God knows what they're thinking about,
but it's certainly not that. Dumping you with a lot of old
people who've hung on for too long and nobody wants
around any more? You're still living your life, Helen, not
drooling it away. The only legal way they can get you out of
this house is by having you certified.

(*Awkward silence.*)

We all know you're as mad as a hatter, but it's not quite
that bad.

(*Another pause.*)

One little question though, Miss Helen. You haven't been
going around talking about doing away with yourself to
anyone have you?

HELEN: I told you, Katrina is the only person I really see any
more.

ELSA: And Marius. Don't forget him. Anyway it doesn't matter
who it is. All it needs is one person to be able to stand up
and testify that they heard you say it.

HELEN: Well, I haven't.

ELSA: Because it would make life a lot easier for them if they
ever did try to do something. So no more of that. OK? Did
you hear me, Helen?

HELEN: Yes, I heard you.

ELSA: And while you're about it, add me to your list. I don't
want to hear or read any more about it either.

HELEN: I heard you, Elsie! Why do you keep on about it?

ELSA: Because talk like that could be grounds for forcibly
committing someone to a 'Sunshine Home for the Aged'!
I'm sorry, Helen, but what do you expect me to do?
Pretend you never said it? Is that what you would have
done if our situations had been reversed? If in the middle of
my mess I had threatened to do that? God knows, I came
near to feeling like it a couple of times. I had a small taste
of how bloody pointless everything can seem to be. But if I
can hang on, then you most certainly can't throw in the
towel – not after all the rounds you've already won against
them. So when the Dominee comes around, you're going to

43

put on a brave front. Let's get him and his stupid ideas about an old-age home right out of your life. Because you're going to say No, remember? Be as polite and civil as you like – we'll offer him tea and biscuits and discuss the weather and the evils of alcohol – but when the time comes, you're going to thank him for all his trouble and consideration and then hand this back to him with a firm 'No, thank you.'

(*Another idea.*)

And just to make quite sure he gets the message, you can also mention your trip into Graaff-Reinet next week to see a doctor and an optician.

HELEN: What do you mean?

ELSA: Exactly what I said: appointments with a doctor and an optician.

HELEN: But I haven't got any.

ELSA: You will on Monday. Before I leave tomorrow I'm going to ask Getruida to take you into Graaff-Reinet next week. And this time you're going to go. There must be something they can do about your hands, even if it's just to ease the pain. And a little 'regmaker' for your depressions.

(MISS HELEN *wants to say something.*)

No arguments! And to hell with your vanity as well. We all know you think you're the prettiest thing in the village, but if you need glasses, you're going to wear them. I'll make the appointments myself and phone through after you've been in to find out what the verdict is. I'm not trying to be funny, Helen. You've got to prove to the village that you are quite capable of looking after yourself. It's the only way to shut them up.

HELEN: You're going too fast for me, Elsa. You're not allowing me to say anything.

ELSA: That's quite right. How many times in the past have we sat down and tried to talk about all of this? And every time the same story: 'I'll think about it, Elsa.' Your thinking has got us nowhere, Helen. This time you're just going to agree . . . and that includes letting Katrina come in a couple of times each week to do the house.

44

HELEN: There's nothing for her to do. I can manage by myself.

ELSA: No, you can't.

(*She runs her finger over a piece of furniture and holds it up for* MISS HELEN *to see the dust.*)

HELEN: Everything would have been spotless if I had known you were coming.

ELSA: It's got to be spotless all the time! To hell with *my* visits and holidays. I don't live here. You do. I'm concerned with *your* life, Helen. And I'm also not blind, you know. I saw you struggling with that large kettle. Yes, let's talk about that. When did you last boil up enough water for a decent bath? Come on, Helen. Can't you remember? Some time ago, right? Is it because of personal neglect that you've stopped caring about yourself or because you aren't able to? Answer me.

HELEN: I can't listen to you any more, Elsa.

(*She makes a move to leave the room.*)

ELSA: Don't do that to me Helen! If you leave this room I'm getting into my car and driving back to Cape Town. You wrote that letter. I haven't made it up. All I'm trying to do is deal with it.

HELEN: No, you're not.

ELSA: Then I give up. What in God's name have we been talking about?

HELEN: A pair of spectacles and medicine for my arthritis and Katrina dusting the house . . .

ELSA: Do you want me to read it again?

HELEN: (*Ignoring the interruption*) You're treating that letter like a shopping list. That isn't what I was writing about.

ELSA: Then what was it?

HELEN: Darkness, Elsa! Darkness!

(*She speaks with an emotional intensity and authority which forces* ELSA *to listen in silence.*)

The Darkness that nearly smothered my life in here one night fifteen years ago. The same Darkness that used to come pouring down the chimney and into the room at night when I was a little girl and frighten me. If you still don't know what I'm talking about, blow out the candles!

But those were easy Darknesses to deal with. The one
I'm talking about now is much worse. It's inside me,
Elsa . . . it's got inside me at last and I can't light candles
there.

(*Pause.*)

I never knew that could happen. I thought I was safe. I had
grown up and I had all the candles I wanted. That is all that
little girl could think about when she lay there in bed,
trying to make her prayers last as long as she could because
she was terrified of the moment when her mother would
bend down and kiss her and take away the candle. One day
she would have her very own! That was the promise: that
one day when I was big enough, she would leave one at my
bedside for me to light as often as I wanted. That's all that
'getting big' ever meant to me – my very own candle at my
bedside.

Such brave little lights! And they taught the little girl
how to be that. When she saw one burning in the middle of
the night, she knew what courage was. All my life they have
helped me to find courage . . . until now.

I'm frightened, Elsie, more frightened than that little girl
ever was. There's no 'getting big' left to wait for, no prayers
to say until that happens . . . and the candles don't help
any more. That is what I was trying to tell you. I'm
frightened. And Marius can see it. He's no fool, Elsa. He
knows that his moment has finally come.

ELSA: What moment?

HELEN: He's been waiting a long time for me to reach the end
of my Mecca. I thought I had cheated him out of it, that
that moment would never come.

All those years when I was working away, when it was
slowly taking shape, he was there as well . . . standing in
the distance, watching and waiting.

I used to peep at him through the curtains. He'd come
walking past, then stop, stand there at the gate with his hands
behind his back and stare at my Wise Men. And even though
he didn't show anything, I know he didn't like what he saw. I
used to sing when I was working. He heard me one

46

day and came up and asked: 'Are you really that happy, Helen?'

I laughed. Not at *him*, believe me not at him, but because I had a secret he would never understand.

(*Pause.*)

It's his turn to laugh now. But he won't, of course. He's not that sort of man. He'll be very gentle again . . . pull the curtains and close the shutters the way he did that night fifteen years ago . . . because nobody must stare into a house where there's been a death.

If my Mecca is finished, Elsa, then so is my life.

(ELSA *is overwhelmed by a sense of helplessness and defeat.*)

ELSA: I think I've had it. It's too much for one day. That woman on the road and now you. I honestly don't know how to handle it. In fact, at this moment, I don't think I know anything. I don't know what it means to be walking eighty miles to Cradock with your baby on your back. I don't know whether your Mecca is finished or not. And all I know about Darkness is that that is when you put on the lights. Jesus! I wouldn't mind somebody coming along and telling me what it does all mean.

So where does all of that leave us, Miss Helen? I'm lost. What are you going to do when he comes?

(*No answer.*)

Ask him – please – for more time? One thing I can tell you right now is that there's no point to that. If you don't say no tonight, you won't ever, in which case you might as well sign that form and get it over and done with.

(*A cruel, relentless tone in her voice.*)

There's no point in talking about anything until that's settled. So you better think about it, Helen. While you do that, I'll see what I can organize for supper.

(*She exits into the kitchen. A man's voice off: 'Anybody at home?' * MARIUS *appears in the doorway.*)

MARIUS: Miss Helen! Alone in the dark? I didn't think anybody was home.

(ELSA *appears from the kitchen.*)

Ah, Miss Barlow!

CURTAIN

The same a few minutes later. MARIUS *and* ELSA *are now at the table with* MISS HELEN, *the centre of attraction being a basket of vegetables which Marius has brought with him. He is about the same age as* MISS HELEN *and is neatly but casually dressed. He speaks with simple sincerity and charm.*

MARIUS: (*Holding up a potato*) Feast your eyes on this, Miss Barlow! A genuine Sneeuberg potato! A pinch of salt and you've got a meal, and if you want to be extravagant, add a little butter and you have indeed got a feast. We had a farmer from the Gamtoos Valley up here last week, trying to sell potatoes to us! Can you believe it? Did you see him, Helen? He had his lorry parked in front of the Post Office. What's the English expression, Miss Barlow? Coals to – where?

ELSA: Coals to Newcastle.

MARIUS: That's it! Well in this case it was very near to being an insult as well. We pride ourselves in these parts on knowing what a potato really is. And here you have it. The 'apple of the earth', as the French would say. But I don't imagine that poor man will come again. Shame! I ended up feeling very sorry for him. 'Don't you people like potatoes?' he asked me. What could I say? I didn't have the heart to tell him he'd wasted his time driving all this distance, that *nobody* comes to the Sneeuberg to sell potatoes! And then, to make me feel really bad, he insisted on giving me a small sack of them before he drove off. I don't think he sold enough to cover the cost of his petrol back home.

I also brought you a few beets and tomatoes. The beets have passed their best now, but if you pickle and bottle them, they'll be more than all right. Have you ever treated our young friend to a taste of that, Miss Helen? (*To* ELSA) It's one of our local specialities. One thing I can assure you ladies is that these vegetables are as fresh as you are ever likely to get. I dug them up myself this afternoon.

HELEN: It's very kind of you, Marius, but you really shouldn't have bothered.

MARIUS: It wasn't any bother at all. I've got more than enough for myself stored away in the pantry. Would have been a sin to leave them to rot in the ground when somebody else could use them. And at our age we need fresh vegetables, Helen. (*Wagging a finger at her*) Marie biscuits and tea are not a balanced diet. (*To* ELSA) In the old days Helen used to have a very fine vegetable garden of her own out there. But as you can see, the humble potato has been crowded out by other things. I don't think there's enough room left out there now to grow a radish.

(*He turns back to the basket.*)

Yes, the Good Lord was very generous to us this past year. I don't really know that we deserve it, but our rains came just when we needed them. Not too much or too little. Believe me, young lady, we are well experienced in both those possibilities. Not so, Helen?

ELSA: The Karoo looked very dry and desolate to me as I drove through it this afternoon.

MARIUS: Dry it certainly is, but not desolate. It might appear that to a townsman's eye – as indeed it did to mine when I first came here! – but that is because we are already deep into our autumn. It will be a good few months before we see rain again.

ELSA: I've never thought of this world as having seasons . . . certainly not the soft ones. To me it has always been a landscape of extremes, too hot or too cold, too dry or else Miss Helen is writing to me about floods that have cut off the village from the outside world. It reminds me of something I once read where the desert was described as 'God without mankind'.

MARIUS: What an interesting thought: 'God without mankind'. I can't decide whether that's Catholic or Protestant. Would you know?

ELSA: (*Shaking her head*) No.

MARIUS: Who wrote it?

ELSA: A French writer. Balzac. It sums up the way I feel about
the Karoo. The Almighty hasn't exactly made mankind
over-welcome here, has he? In fact, it almost looks as if he
resented our presence. Sorry, Dominee, I don't mean to be
blasphemous or ungenerous to your world, it's just that I'm
used to a gentler one.

MARIUS: You judge it too harshly, Miss Barlow. It has got its
gentle moments and moods as well . . . all the more
precious because there are so few of them. We can't afford
to take them for granted. As you can see, it feeds us. Can
any man or woman ask for more than that from the little bit
of earth he lives on?

ELSA: Do you think your Coloured folk feel the same way about
things?

MARIUS: Why should it be any different for them?

ELSA: I was just wondering whether they had as many reasons to
be as contented as you?

MARIUS: I was talking about simple gratitude, Miss Barlow.
Wouldn't you say contentment is a more complicated state
of mind? One that can very easily be disturbed. But
grateful? Yes! Our Coloured folk also have every reason to
be. Ask them. Ask little Katrina, who visits Miss Helen so
faithfully, if she or her baby have ever wanted for food . . .
even when Koos has spent all his wages on liquor. There
are no hungry people, white or coloured, in this village,
Miss Barlow. Those of us who are more fortunate than
others are well aware of the responsibilities that go with that
good fortune. But I don't want to get into an argument. It
is my world—and Helen's—and we can't expect an outsider
to love or understand it as we do.

ELSA: I'll put these (*the vegetables*) away for you, Miss Helen.

MARIUS: Don't bother to unpack them now. I'll collect the
basket tomorrow after church.

(*Calling after* ELSA *as she leaves the room:*)
And there's no need to wash them. I've already done that.
Just put them straight into the pot.

(*Exit* ELSA.)

51

I've got a feeling that, given half a chance, your young friend and myself *could* very easily find ourselves in an argument. I think Miss Barlow gets a little impatient with our old-fashioned ways and attitudes. But it's too late for us to change now. Right, Helen?

HELEN: Elsa and I have already had those arguments, Marius.

MARIUS: I hope you put up a good defence on our behalf.

HELEN: I tried my best.

MARIUS: And yet the two of you still remain good friends.

HELEN: Oh yes!

MARIUS: And so it should be. A true friendship should be able to accommodate a difference of opinion. You didn't mention anything about her coming up for a visit last time we talked.

HELEN: Because I didn't know. It's an unexpected visit.

MARIUS: Will she be staying long?

HELEN: Just tonight. She goes back tomorrow.

MARIUS: Good heavens! All this way for only one night. I hope nothing is wrong.

HELEN: No. She just decided on the spur of the moment to visit me. But she's got to go back because they're very busy at school. They're right in the middle of exams.

MARIUS: I see. May I sit down for a moment, Helen?

HELEN: Of course, Marius. Forgive me, I'm forgetting my manners.

MARIUS: I won't stay long. I must put down a few thoughts for tomorrow's sermon. And, thanks to you, I know what I want to say.

HELEN: Me?

MARIUS: Yes, you. (*Teasing her:*) You are responsible . . .

HELEN: Oh dear!

MARIUS: (*A little laugh*) Relax, Helen. I only said 'thanks to you' because it came to me this afternoon while I was digging up your vegetables. I spent a lot of time, while I was out in the garden doing that, just leaning on my spade. My back is giving me a bit of trouble again and, to tell you the truth, I also felt lazy.

I wasn't thinking about anything in particular . . . just

52

looking, you know, the way an old man does, looking around, recognizing once again and saying the names. Spitskop in the distance! Aasvoelkrans down at the other end of the valley. The poplars with their autumn foliage standing around as yellow and still as that candle flame!

And a lot of remembering.

As you know, Helen, I had deep and very painful wounds in my soul when I first came here. Wounds I thought would never heal. This was going to be where I finally escaped from life, turned my back on it and justified what was left of my existence by ministering to you people's simple needs. I was very wrong. I didn't escape life here, I discovered it, what it really means, the fullness and goodness of it. It's a deep and lasting regret that Aletta wasn't alive to share that discovery with me. Anyway, all of this was going on in my head when I realized I was hearing a small little voice, and the small little voice was saying, 'Thank you.' With every spadeful of earth that I turned when I went down on my knees to lift the potatoes out of the soil, there it was: 'thank you.' It was mine! I was muttering away to myself the way we old folks are inclined to do when nobody is around. It was me saying, 'Thank you.'

That is what I want to do tomorrow, Helen. Give thanks, but in a way that I've never done before.

I know I've stood there in the pulpit many times telling all of you to do exactly that, but oh dear me, the cleverness and conceit in the soul of Marius Byleveld when he was doing that! I had an actor's vanity up there, Helen. I'm not saying I was a total hypocrite but, believe me, in those thanksgivings I was listening to my Dominee's voice and its hoped-for eloquence every bit as much as to the true little voice inside my heart . . . the voice I heard so clearly this afternoon.

That's the voice that must speak tomorrow! And to do that I must find words as simple as the sky I was standing under this afternoon or the earth I was turning over with my spade. They have got no vanities and conceits. They are

53

just 'there'. If the Almighty takes pity on us, the one gives us rain so that the other can in turn . . . give us this day our daily potato. (*A smile at this gentle little joke.*) Am I making sense, Helen? Answer me truthfully.

HELEN: Yes, you are, Marius. And if all you do tomorrow is say what you have just said to me, it will be very moving and beautiful.

MARIUS: (*Sincerely*) Truly, Helen? Do you really mean that?

HELEN: Every word of it.

MARIUS: Then I will try.

My twentieth anniversary comes up next month. Yes, that is how long I've been here. Twenty-one years ago, on May the sixteenth, the Good Lord called my Aletta to his side, and just over a year later, on June the eleventh, I gave my first sermon in New Bethesda. (*A little laugh at the memory.*) What an occasion that was!

I don't know if I showed it, Helen, but let me confess now that I was more than just a little nervous when I went up into the pulpit and looked down at that stern and formidable array of faces. A very different proposition from the town and city congregations I had been preaching to up until then. When Miss de Klerk played the first bars of the hymn at the end of it, I heaved a very deep sigh of relief. None of you had fallen asleep!

(HELEN *is shaking her head.*)

What's the matter?

HELEN: Young Miss de Klerk came later. Mrs Niewoudt was still our organist when you gave your first service.

MARIUS: Are you sure?

HELEN: Yes. Mrs Niewoudt also played at the reception we gave you afterwards in Mr van Heerden's house. She played the piano and Sterling Retief sang.

MARIUS: You know something, I do believe you're right! Good heavens, Helen, your memory is better than mine.

HELEN: And you had no cause to be nervous. You were very impressive.

MARIUS: (*A small pause as he remembers something else*) Yes, of course. You were in that congregation. Stefanus was at your

54

side, as he was going to be every Sunday after that for . . .
what? Another five years?

HELEN: Five years.

MARIUS: That was all a long time ago.

HELEN: More than a long time, Marius. It feels like another life.
(ELSA *returns with a tray of tea and sandwiches.*)

MARIUS: Ah, here comes your supper. I must be running along.

ELSA: Just a sandwich, Dominee. Neither of us is very hungry.

MARIUS: I'll drop by tomorrow night if that is all right with
you, Helen.

ELSA: Won't you have a cup of tea with us? It's the least we can
offer in return for all those lovely vegetables.

MARIUS: I don't want to intrude. Helen tells me you're here for
just the night, Miss Barlow. I'm sure you ladies have got
things to talk about in private.

ELSA: We've already done quite a lot of that, haven't we, Helen?
Please don't go because of me. I have some school work I
must see to. I'll take my tea through to the other room.

HELEN: Don't go, Elsa!

ELSA: I told you I had papers to mark, Miss Helen. I'll just get
on with that quietly while the two of you have a little chat.

HELEN: Please!

ELSA: All right then, if it will make you happier, I'll bring my
work through and do it in here.

MARIUS: No. I've obviously come at an inconvenient time.

ELSA: Not at all, Dominee. Miss Helen was expecting you.
(ELSA *fetches the application form for the old-age home and
puts it down on the table. A moment between* ELSA *and*
MARIUS. *He turns to* HELEN *for confirmation.*)

HELEN: Yes, I was.

ELSA: How do you like your tea?

MARIUS: Very well, if you insist. Milk but no sugar, please.
(ELSA *pours tea, then collects her briefcase from the bedroom
alcove and settles down to work at a small table at the back of
the room.*)
You're quite certain you want to discuss this now, Helen?

HELEN: Yes, Marius.

MARIUS: It can wait until tomorrow.

HELEN: No, I'm ready.

MARIUS: Right. Just before we start talking, Helen, the good
news is that I've spoken to Dominee Gericke in
Graaff-Reinet again, and the room is definitely yours – that
is, if you want it, of course. But they obviously can't have it
standing empty indefinitely. As it is, he's already broken
the rules by putting you at the top of the waiting list, but as
a personal favour. He understands the circumstances. So
the sooner we decide, one way or the other, the better. But
I want you to know that I do realize how big a move it is for
you. I want you to be quite certain and happy in your mind
that you're doing the right thing. So don't think we've got
to rush into it, start packing up immediately or anything
like that. A decision must be made, one way or the other,
but once you've done that, you can relax and take all the
time you need.

(MARIUS *takes spectacles, a little notebook, pen and pencil
from a jacket pocket. The way he handles everything, carefully
and precisely, reveals a meticulous and orderly mind. He opens
the application form.* MISS HELEN *gives* ELSA *the first of many
desperate and appealing looks.* ELSA, *engrossed in her work,
apparently does not notice it.* MARIUS *puts his spectacles on.*)

I know we went over this the last time, but there still are
just a few questions. Yes . . . we put Stefanus's father's
name down as Petrus Johannes Martins, but in the Church
registry it's down as Petrus *Jacobus*.

(*He takes his spectacles off.*)

Which one is correct, Helen? Can you remember? You were
so certain of Petrus Johannes last time.

HELEN: I still am. But what did you say the other one was?

MARIUS: Petrus Jacobus.

HELEN: Jacobus . . . Johannes . . . No, maybe I'm not.

MARIUS: In that case what I think I will do is enter it as Petrus
J. Martins. Just as well I checked.

(*He puts his spectacles on again and turns back to the form.*)

And next . . . yes, the date of your confirmation. Have you
been able to find the certificate?

HELEN: No, I haven't. I'm sorry, Marius. I did look, but I'm afraid my papers are all in a mess.

MARIUS: (*Taking his spectacles off*) I've been through the church records, but I can't find anything that sheds any light on it. It's not all that important, of course, but it would have been nice to have had that date as well.

(*He replaces his spectacles.*)

Let's see . . . what shall we do? You think you were about twelve?

HELEN: Something like that.

MARIUS: What I'll do is just pencil in 1920 and have one more look. I hate giving up on *that* one. But you surprise me, Helen – of all the dates to have forgotten.

That takes care of the form now.

(*He consults his notebook.*)

Yes. Two little points from Dominee Gericke, after which you can relax and enjoy your supper. He asked me – and do believe me, Helen, he was just trying to be practical and helpful, nothing else – whether you had taken care of everything by way of a last will and testament, and obviously I said I didn't know.

HELEN: What do you mean, Marius?

MARIUS: That in the event of something happening, your house and possessions will be disposed of in the way that you want them to be. Have you done that?

HELEN: I've still got a copy of Stefanus's will. He left everything to me.

MARIUS: We're talking about you, Helen. Have you seen a lawyer?

HELEN: No, I . . . I've never thought of it.

MARIUS: Then it is just as well Gericke asked. Believe me, Helen, in my time as a minister I have seen so many bitterly unhappy situations because somebody neglected to look after that side of things. Families not talking to each other! Lawsuits over a few pieces of furniture! I really do think it is something you should see to. We're at an age now when anything can happen. I had mine revised only a few months ago.

(*He glances at the notebook again.*)

57

And finally, he made the obvious suggestion that we arrange for you to visit the home as soon as possible. Just to meet the Matron and other people there and to see your room. He's particularly anxious for you to see it so that you know what you need to bring on your side. He had a dreadful to-do a few months ago with a lady who tried to move a whole houseful of furniture into her little room. Don't get worried, though. There's plenty of space for personal possessions and a few of your . . . ornaments. That covers everything, I think. All that's left now is for you to sign it . . . provided you want to do that, of course. (*He places his fountain pen, in readiness, on the form.*)

HELEN: Marius . . . please . . . please can I talk for a little bit now?

MARIUS: But of course, Helen.

HELEN: I've done a lot of thinking since we last spoke . . .

MARIUS: Good! We both agreed that was necessary. This is not a step to be taken lightly.

HELEN: Yes, I've done a lot of thinking, and I've worked out a plan.

MARIUS: For what, Helen?

HELEN: A plan to take care of everything.

MARIUS: Excellent!

HELEN: I'm going in to Graaff-Reinet next week, Marius, to see a doctor. I'm going to make the appointment on Monday, and I'll ask Getruida to drive me in.

MARIUS: You make it sound serious, Helen.

HELEN: No, it's just my arthritis. I'm going to get some medicine for it.

MARIUS: For a moment you had me worried. I thought the burns were possibly more serious than we had realized. But why not save yourself a few pennies and see Dr Lubbe at the home? He looks after everybody there free of charge.

HELEN: (*Hanging on*) And spectacles. I'm also going to make arrangements to see an optician and get a pair of spectacles.

MARIUS: Splendid, Helen! You certainly have been making plans.

HELEN: And, finally, I've decided to get Katrina to come in two

58

or three times a week to help me with the house.

MARIUS: Katrina?

HELEN: Little Katrina. Koos Malgas's wife.

MARIUS: I know who you're talking about, Helen. It's just . . . oh dear! I'm sorry to be the one to tell you this, Helen, but I think you are going to lose your little Katrina.

HELEN: What do you mean, Marius?

MARIUS: Koos has asked the Divisional Council for a transfer to their Aberdeen depot, and I think he will get it.

HELEN: So?

MARIUS: I imagine Katrina and the baby will go with him.

HELEN: Katrina . . . ?

MARIUS: Will be leaving the village.

HELEN: No, it can't be.

MARIUS: It's the truth, Helen.

HELEN: But she's said nothing to me about it. She was in here just a few days ago and she didn't mention anything about leaving.

MARIUS: She most probably didn't think it important.

HELEN: How can you say that, Marius? Of course it is! She knows how much I depend on her. If Katrina goes, I'll be completely alone here except for you and the times when Elsa is visiting.

(MISS HELEN *is becoming increasingly distressed.*)

MARIUS: Come now, Helen! It's not as bad as that. I know Katrina is a sweet little soul and that you are very fond of her, as we all are, but don't exaggerate things. There are plenty of good women in the location who can come and give you a hand in here and help you pack up . . . if you decide to move. Tell you what I'll do: if you're worried about a stranger being in here with all your personal things, I'll lend you my faithful old Nonna. She's been looking after me for ten years now, and in that time I haven't missed a single thing. You could trust her with your life.

HELEN: I'm not talking about a servant, Marius.

MARIUS: I thought we were.

HELEN: Katrina is the only friend I've got left in the village.

MARIUS: That's a hard thing you're saying, Helen. All of us still like to think of ourselves as your friends.

HELEN: I wasn't including you, Marius. You're different. But as for the others . . . no. They've all become strangers to me. I might just as well not know their names. And they treat me as if I were a stranger to them as well.

MARIUS: You're being very unfair, Helen. They behave towards you in the way you apparently want them to, which is to leave you completely alone. Really, Helen! Strangers? Old Getruida, Sterling, Jerry, Boet, Mrs van Heerden? You grew up in this village with all of them.

To be very frank, Helen, it's your manner which now keeps them at a distance. I don't think you realize how much you've changed over the years. You're not easily recognizable to others any more as the person they knew fifteen years ago. And then your hobby, if I can call it that, hasn't really helped matters. This is not exactly the sort of room the village ladies are used to or would feel comfortable in having afternoon tea. As for all of that out there . . . the less said about it, the better.

HELEN: I don't harm or bother anyone, Marius!

MARIUS: And does anyone harm or bother you?

HELEN: Yes! Everybody is trying to force me to leave my home.

MARIUS: Nobody is *forcing* you, Helen! In Heaven's name, where do you get that idea from? If you sign this form, it must be of your own free will.

You're very agitated tonight, Helen. Has something happened to upset you? You were so reasonable about everything the last time we talked. You seemed to understand that the only motive on our side is to try and do what is best for you. And even then it's only in the way of advice. We can't *tell* you what to do. But if you want us to stop caring about what happens to you, we can try . . . though I don't know how our Christian consciences would allow us to do that.

HELEN: I don't believe the others care about me, Marius. All they want is to get rid of me. This village has also changed over the past fifteen years. I am not alone in that. I don't recognize it any more as the simple, innocent world I grew up in.

MARIUS: If it's as bad as that, Helen, if you are now really that unhappy and lonely here, then I don't know why you have any doubts about leaving.

(MISS HELEN's *emotional state has deteriorated steadily. Marius's fountain pen has ended up in her hand. She looks down at the application form. A few seconds' pause and then a desperate cry.*)

HELEN: Why don't you stop me, Elsa! I'm going to sign it!

ELSA: (*Abandoning all pretence of being absorbed in her work*) Then go ahead and do it! Sign that fucking form. If that's what you want to do to your life, just get it over and done with, for God's sake!

MARIUS: Miss Barlow!

ELSA: (*Ignoring him*) What are you waiting for, Helen? You're wasting our time. It's late and we want to go to bed.

HELEN: But you said I mustn't sign it.

ELSA: (*Brutally*) I've changed my mind. Do it. Hurry up and dispose of your life so that we can get on with ours.

HELEN: Stop it, Elsa. Help me. Please help me.

ELSA: Sorry, Helen. I've had more woman-battering today than I can cope with. You can at least say no. That woman on the road couldn't. But if you haven't got the guts to do that, then too bad. I'm not going to do it for you.

HELEN: I tried.

ELSA: You call that trying? All it required was one word – no.

HELEN: Please believe me, Elsa . . . I was trying!

ELSA: No good, Helen. If that's your best, then maybe you will be better off in an old-age home.

MARIUS: Gently, Miss Barlow! In Heaven's name, gently! What's got into you?

ELSA: Exhaustion, Dominee. Very near total mental and emotional exhaustion, to the point where I want to scream. I've already done that once today, and right now I wouldn't mind doing it a second time. Yes, Helen, I've had it. Why were you 'crying out to me in the dark'? To be an audience when you signed away your life? Is that why I'm here? Twelve hours of driving like a lunatic for that? God. What a

61

farce! I might just as well have stayed in Cape Town.

MARIUS: Maybe it's a pity you didn't. I think I understand now why Helen is so agitated tonight. But unfortunately you are here, and if you've got anything to say to her, in Heaven's name be considerate of the state she is in. She needs help, not to be confused and terrified even more.

ELSA: Helen understands the way I feel. We *did* do a lot of talking before you came, Dominee.

MARIUS: I'm concerned with *her* feelings, Miss Barlow, not yours. And if by any chance you are as well, then try to show some respect for her age. Helen is a much older woman than you. You were shouting at her as if she was a child.

ELSA: Me, treating her like a child? Oh my God! You can stand there and accuse me of that after what I've just seen and heard from you?

MARIUS: I don't know what you're talking about.

ELSA: Then I'll tell you. You were doing everything in your power to bully and blackmail her into signing that. You were taking the grossest advantage of what you call her confusion and helplessness. I've been trying to tell her she's neither confused nor helpless.

MARIUS: So you know what is best for her.

ELSA: No, no, no! Wrong again, Dominee. I think *she* does. And if you had given her half a chance, she would have told you that that is not being dumped in an old-age home full of old people who have reached the end of their lives. She hasn't. You forget one thing: I didn't stop her signing that form. She stopped herself.

MARIUS: It was a moment of confusion.

ELSA: There you go again! Can't you leave that word alone? She is not confused!

MARIUS: When Helen and I discussed the matter a few days ago . . .

ELSA: Don't talk about her as if she were not here. She's right next to you, Dominee. Ask her, for God's sake . . . but this time give her a chance to answer.

MARIUS: Don't try to goad me with blasphemy, Miss Barlow.

I'm beginning to think Helen needs as much protection
from you as she does from herself.

ELSA: You still haven't asked her.

MARIUS: Because I have some sympathy for her condition.
Look at her! She is in no condition now, thanks to you, to
think clearly about anything.

ELSA: She was an emotional mess, thanks to you, before I
opened my mouth. Don't expect me to believe you really
care about her.

MARIUS: (*Trying hard to control himself*) Miss Barlow, for the last
time, what you do or don't believe is not of the remotest
concern to me. Helen is, and my concern is that she gets a
chance to live out what is left of her life as safely and
happily as is humanly possible. I don't think that should
include the danger of her being trapped in here when this
house goes up in flames.

ELSA: What are you talking about?

MARIUS: Her accident. The night she knocked over the candle.
(ELSA *is obviously at a loss.*)
You don't know about that? When was it, Helen? Four
weeks ago?
(*Pause.* MISS HELEN *doesn't respond.*)
I see. You didn't tell your friend about your narrow escape.
I think I owe you an apology, Miss Barlow. I assumed you
knew all about it.

ELSA: You owe me nothing. Just tell me what happened.

MARIUS: Yes, it was about four weeks ago. Helen knocked over
a candle one night and set fire to the curtains. I try not to
think about what would have happened if Sterling hadn't
been looking out of his window at that moment and seen
the flames. He rushed over, and just in time. She had
stopped trying to put out the flames herself and was just
standing staring at them. Even so she picked up a few bad
burns on her hands. We had to get Sister Lategan out of
bed to treat them. But it could have been a lot worse.
(ELSA *is staring at* MISS HELEN.)
We don't want that on our consciences. So you see, Miss
Barlow, our actions are not quite as pointless or as uncaring

63

as they must have seemed to you.

ELSA: One of the lamps started smoking badly, and there was a little accident at the stove while you were making prickly-pear syrup for me! Oh boy! You certainly can do it, Helen. Don't let us ever again talk about trust between the two of us. Anyway, that settles it. I leave the two of you to fight it out . . . and may the best man win! I'm going to bed.

HELEN: Give me a chance to explain.

ELSA: (*Ignoring the plea*) Good night. See you in the morning. I'll be making an early start, Helen.

HELEN: Don't abandon me, Elsa!

ELSA: You've abandoned yourself, Helen! Don't accuse me of that! You were the first to jump overboard. You haven't got enough faith in your life and your work to defend them against him. You lied to me . . . and such stupid bloody lies! What was the point? For that matter, what is the point of anything? Why *did* you make me come up? And then all our talk about trust! God, what a joke. You've certainly made me make a fool of myself again, but this time I don't think it's funny. In fact, I fucking well resent it.

HELEN: I didn't tell you because I was frightened you would agree with them.

ELSA: Don't say anything, Helen. You're making it worse.
(*She studies* MISS HELEN *with cruel detachment.*)
But you might have a point there. Now that I've heard about your 'little accident', I'm beginning to think they might be right.
(*She indicates the room.*)
Corrugated iron and wooden walls? Give it half a chance and this would go up like a bonfire.
(*She is hating herself, hurting herself every bit as much as she is hurting* MISS HELEN, *but is unable to stop.*)
And he says you were just standing and staring at it. What was that all about? Couldn't you make a run for it? They say that about terror – it makes you either run like hell or stand quite still. Sort of paralysis. Because it was just an accident, wasn't it, Helen? I mean, you weren't trying

anything else, were you? Spite everybody by taking the house with you in a final blaze of glory! Dramatic! But it's a hell of a way to go. There are easier methods.

(MISS HELEN *goes up to* ELSA *and stares at her.*)

HELEN: Who are you?

(*The question devastates* ELSA.)

MARIUS: Ladies, ladies, enough! Stop now! I don't know what's going on between the two of you, but in Heaven's name stop it. I think Helen is aware of the dangers involved, Miss Barlow. And now that you do as well, can't we appeal to you to add your weight to ours and help persuade her to do the right thing? As I am sure you now realize, our only concern has been her well-being.

ELSA: You want my help.

MARIUS: Yes. If now at last you understand why we were trying to persuade Helen to move to the home, then on her behalf I am indeed appealing to you. We don't persecute harmless old ladies, Miss Barlow.

ELSA: And one that isn't so harmless?

MARIUS: Now what are you trying to say?

ELSA: That Helen isn't harmless, Dominee. Anything but that. That's why you people can't leave her alone.

MARIUS: For fifteen years we have done exactly that.

ELSA: Stoning her house and statues at night is not leaving her alone. That is not the way you treat a harmless old lady.

MARIUS: In Heaven's name! Are you going to drag that up? Those were children, Miss Barlow, and it was a long, long time ago. It has not happened again. Do you really mean to be that unfair? Can't you bring as much understanding as you claim to have of Helen's situation to a few other things as well? You've seen what is out there . . .

(*He gestures at the window and Miss Helen's 'Mecca'.*)

How else do you expect the simple children of the village to react to all that? It frightens them, Miss Barlow. I'm not joking! Think back to your impressionable years as a little girl. I know for a fact that all the children in the village believe this house is haunted and that ghosts walk around out there at night. Don't scoff at them. I'm sure there were

65

monsters and evil spirits in your childhood as well. But as I said, that was all a long, long time ago. The moment we discovered what they were doing, we in turn did everything we could to put a stop to it. Mr Lategan, the school principal, and I both lectured them in the sternest possible manner. Come now, Miss Barlow, have you learned nothing about us in the course of the few years that you've been visiting the village?

ELSA: A lot more than I would have liked to. Those children didn't arrive at their attitude to Helen on their own. I've also heard about the parents who frighten naughty children with stories about Miss Helen's 'monsters'. They got the courage to start throwing stones because of what they had heard their mothers and fathers saying. And as far as *they* are concerned, Helen is anything but a harmless old lady. God, what an irony. We spend our time talking about 'poor, frightened Miss Helen', whereas it's all of you who are really frightened.

MARIUS: I can only repeat what I've already said to Helen: the people you are talking about grew up with her and have known her a lot longer than you.

ELSA: Not any more. You also said that, remember? That stopped fifteen years ago when she didn't resign herself to being the meek, church-going little widow you all expected her to be. Instead she did something which small minds and small souls can never forgive . . . she dared to be different! Which does make you right about one thing, Dominee. Those statues out there *are* monsters. And they are that for the simple reason that they express Helen's freedom. Yes, I never thought it was a word you would like. I'm sure it ranks as a cardinal sin in these parts. A free woman! God forgive us!

Have you ever wondered why I come up here? It's a hell of a long drive, you know, if the only reason is sympathy for a lonely old lady whom nobody is talking to any more. And it's also not for the scenery.

She challenges me, Dominee. She challenges me into an awareness of myself and my life, of my responsibilities to both that I never had until I met her. There's a hell of a lot

66

of talk about freedom, and all sorts of it, in the world where I come from. But it's mostly talk, Dominee, easy talk and nothing else. Not with Helen. She's lived it. One dusty afternoon five years ago, when I came walking down that road hoping for nothing more than to get away from the flies that were driving me mad, I met the first truly free spirit I have ever known.

(*She looks at* MISS HELEN.)

It is her betrayal of all of that tonight that has made me behave the way I have.

(*A pause.* MARIUS *has been confronted with something he has never had to deal with before.*)

MARIUS: You call that . . . that nightmare out there an expression of freedom?

ELSA: Yes. Scary, isn't it? What did you call it earlier? Her hobby?

(*She laughs.*)

Oh no, Dominee. It's much more dangerous than that . . . and I think you know it.

MARIUS: In another age and time it might have been called idolatry.

ELSA: Did you hear that, Helen? (*To* MARIUS) You know what you've just said, don't you?

MARIUS: (*Total conviction*) Oh yes . . . yes, indeed I do. I am also choosing my words very carefully, Miss Barlow.

When I first realized that it was my duty as a friend and a Christian to raise the question with Helen of a move to an old-age home, I decided I would do so on the basis of her physical well-being and safety and nothing else. Helen will tell you that that is all we have ever talked about. I came here tonight meaning once again to do only that. But you have raised other issues, chosen to talk about more than that . . . which forces me now to do so as well. Because there is a lot more than Helen's physical well-being that has worried me, Miss Barlow – and gravely so! Those 'expressions of freedom' have crowded out more than just a few fresh vegetables. I do not take them lightly any more.

I remember the first one very clearly, Helen. I made the mistake of smiling at it, dismissing it as an idle whim coming out of your loneliness. In fact, I think that is how you yourself described it to me, as something to pass away the time. I was very wrong, wasn't I? And very slow in realizing what was really happening. I only began to feel uneasy about it all that first Sunday you weren't in church.

The moment I stood up there in front of the congregation, I knew your place was empty. But even then, you see, I thought you were sick. After the service I hurried around here, but instead of being in bed there you were outside in the yard making yet another . . . (*At a loss for words*) . . . I don't really know what to call them.

HELEN: (*A small but calm voice. She is very still*) It was an owl, Marius. My first owl.

MARIUS: It couldn't have waited until after the service, Helen?

HELEN: Oh no! (*Quietly emphatic*) The picture had come to me in here the night before. I just had to go to work immediately while it was still fresh in my mind. They don't last long, Marius. After a little while it becomes very hard to remember clearly what you saw. I tried explaining to Elsa how it all works . . . but I don't suppose any of you will ever understand.

But don't ever think that missing church that Sunday was something I did lightly, Marius. You don't break the habit of a lifetime without realizing that that life will never quite be the same again. I was already dressed and ready! I had my Bible and hymn book, I was on the point of leaving this room as I had done every Sunday for as long as I could remember . . . but I knew that if I did, I would never make that owl . . . I think I also knew that if I didn't, that if I put aside my Bible and hymn book, took off my hat and changed my dress and went to work . . . Yes! That was my very first owl!

MARIUS: Helen, Helen! I grieve for you! You turned your back on your Church, on your faith and then on us for that? Do you realize that that is why you are now in trouble and so helplessly alone? Those statues out there can't give you love or take care of you the way we wanted to. And, God knows, we were ready to do that. But you spurned us, Helen. You turned your back on our love and left us for the company of those cement monstrosities.

(ELSA, *who has been listening and watching quietly, begins to understand.*)

ELSA: Helen, listen to me. Listen to me carefully because if you understand what I'm going to say, I think everything will be all right.

They're not only frightened of you, Helen; they're also jealous. It's not just the statues that have frightened them. They were throwing stones at something much bigger than that – you. Your life, your beautiful, light-filled, glittering life. And they can't leave it alone, Helen, because they are so, so jealous of it.

HELEN: (*Calmly*) Is that true, Marius?

MARIUS: Helen, has your trust in me been eroded away to the extent that you can ask me that? Does she have so much power over you that you will now believe anything she says?

HELEN: Then . . . it isn't true?

MARIUS: Dear God, what is there left for me to say or do that will make you listen to me the way you do to her?

HELEN: But I have been listening to you, Marius.

MARIUS: No, you haven't! If that were so, you wouldn't be asking me to defend myself against the accusations of someone who knows nothing, nothing, about my true feelings for you. I feel as if I were on trial, Helen. For what? For caring about you?

(*He confronts* MISS HELEN.)

That I am frightened of what you have done to yourself and your life, yes, that is true! When I find that the twenty years we have known each other, all that we have shared in that time, are outweighed by a handful of visits from her, then yes again. That leaves me bewildered and jealous. Don't you realize that you are being used, Helen – she as much as admitted to that – to prove some lunatic notion about freedom? And since we're talking about it, yes yet again, I *do* hate that word. You aren't free, Helen. If anything, exactly the opposite. Don't let her deceive you. If there is one last thing you will let me do for you, then let it be this: see yourself as I do and tell me if that is what you call being 'free'. A life I care about as deeply as any I have known, trapped now finally in the nightmare this house has become . . . with an illiterate little Coloured girl and a stranger from a different world as your only visitors and friends! I know I'm not welcome in here any more. I can feel it the moment I walk in. It's unnatural, Helen. Your life has become as grotesque as those creations of yours out there.

Why, Helen? Why? I will take that question with me to my grave. What possessed you to abandon the life you had, your faith?

HELEN: What life, Marius? What faith? The one that brought me to church every Sunday? (*Shaking her head*) No. You were much too late if you only started worrying about that on the first Sunday I wasn't there in my place. The worst had happened long, long before that. Yes. All those years when, as Elsa said, I sat there so obediently next to Stefanus, it was all a terrible, terrible lie. I tried hard, Marius, but your sermons, the prayers, the hymns, they had all become just words. And there came a time when even they lost their meaning.

Do you know what the word 'God' looks like when you've lost your faith? It looks like a little stone, a cold, round, little stone. 'Heaven' is another one, but its got an awkward, useless shape, while 'Hell' is flat and smooth. All of them – damnation, grace, salvation – a handful of stones.

MARIUS: Why didn't you come to me, Helen? If only you had trusted me enough to tell me, and we had faced it together, I would have broken my soul to help you win back that faith.

HELEN: It felt too late. I'd accepted it. Nothing more was going to happen to me except time and the emptiness inside and I had got used to that . . . until the night in here after Stefanus's funeral.

(*Pause.* MISS HELEN *makes a decision.*)

I've never told you about that night, Marius. I've told no one, not even Elsa, because it was a secret, you see, a very special one, and it had to stay that way while I was working on my Mecca. But so much has happened here tonight, it feels right to do so now.

(*Pause.*)

You brought me home from the cemetery, remember, and when we had got inside the house and you had helped me off with my coat, you put on the kettle for a pot of tea and then . . . ever so thoughtfully . . . pulled the curtains and closed the shutters. Such a small little thing, and I know that you meant well by it, that you didn't want people to stare in at me and my grief . . . but in doing that it felt as if you were putting away my life as surely as the undertaker had done to Stefanus a little earlier when he closed the coffin lid. There was even an odour of death in here with us, wasn't there, sitting in the gloom and talking, both of us in black, our Bibles in our laps? Your words of comfort didn't help. But that wasn't your fault. You didn't know I wasn't mourning Stefanus's death. He was a good man, and it was very sad that he had died so young, but I never loved him. My black widowhood was really for my own life, Marius. While Stefanus was alive there had at least been some pretence at it . . . of a life I hadn't lived. But with him gone . . . ! You had a little girl in here with you, Marius, who had used up all the prayers she knew and was dreading the moment when her mother would bend down, blow out the candle and leave her in the dark. You lit one for me before you left – there was a lot of darkness in this room – and after you had gone I sat here with it. Such a sad little light, with its little tears of wax running down the side! I had none. Neither for Stefanus nor for myself. You see, nothing hurt any more. That little candle did all the crying in here that night, and it burned down very low while doing that. I don't know how much time had passed, but I was just sitting here staring into its flame. I had surrendered myself to what was going to happen when it went out . . . but then instead of doing the same, allowing the darkness to defeat it, that small, uncertain little light seemed to find its courage again. It started to get brighter

71

and brighter. I didn't know whether I was awake any longer or dreaming because a strange feeling came over me . . . that it was leading me . . . leading me far away to a place I had never been to before.

(*She looks around the room and speaks with authority.*)

Light the candles, Elsa. That one first.

(*She indicates a candelabra that has been set up very prominently on a little table.* ELSA *lights it.*)

And you know why, Marius? That is the East. Go out there into the yard and you'll see that all my Wise Men and their camels are travelling in that direction. Follow that candle on and one day you'll come to Mecca. Oh yes, Marius, it's true! I've done it. That is where I went that night and it was the candle you lit that led me there.

(*She is radiantly alive with her vision.*)

A city, Marius! A city of light and colour more splendid than anything I had ever imagined. There were palaces and beautiful buildings everywhere, with dazzling white walls and glittering minarets. Strange statues filled the courtyards. The streets were crowded with camels and turbaned men speaking a language I didn't understand, but that didn't matter because I knew, oh I just knew, it was Mecca! And I was on my way to the grand temple.

In the centre of Mecca there is a temple, Marius, and in the centre of the temple is a vast room with hundreds of mirrors on the walls and hanging lamps, and that is where the Wise Men of the East study the celestial geometry of light and colour. I became an apprentice that night.

Light them all, Elsa, so that I can show Marius what I've learned!

(ELSA *moves around the room lighting all the candles, and as she does so its full magic and splendour is revealed.* MISS HELEN *laughs ecstatically.*)

Look, Marius! Look! Light. Don't be nervous. It's harmless. It only wants to play. That is what I do in here. We play with it like children with a magical toy that never ceases to delight and amuse. Light just one little candle in here, let in the light from just one little star, and the dancing starts. I've even taught it how to skip around corners. Yes, I have! When I lie in bed and look in *that* mirror I can see *that* mirror, and in *that* one the full moon when it rises over the Sneeuberg *behind* my back! This is my world and I have banished darkness from it.

It is not madness, Marius. They say mad people can't tell the difference between what is real and what is not. I can. I know my little Mecca out there, and this room, for what they really are. I had to learn how to bend rusty wire into the right shape and mix sand cement to make my Wise Men and their camels, how to grind down beer bottles in a coffee mill to put glitter on my walls. My hands will never let me forget. They'll keep me sane. It's the best I could do, as near as I could get to the real Mecca. The journey is over now. This is as far as I can go.

I won't be using this (*the application form*). I can't reduce my world to a few ornaments in a small room in an old-age home.

(MARIUS *takes the form. When he speaks again we sense a defeated man, an acceptance of the inevitable behind the quiet attempt to maintain his dignity.*)

MARIUS: Mecca! So that's where you went. I'll look for it on my atlas of the world when I get home tonight. That's a long way away, Helen! I didn't realize you had travelled that far from me. So to find you I must light a candle and follow it to the East!

(*He makes a helpless gesture.*)

No. I think I'm too old now for that journey . . . and I have a feeling that you will never come back.

HELEN: I'm also too old for another journey, Marius. It's taken me my whole life to get here.

I know I've disappointed you—most probably, bitterly so—but, whatever you do, please believe me that it wasn't intentional. I had as little choice over all that has happened as I did over the day I was born.

MARIUS: No, I think I do believe you, Helen . . . which only makes it all the harder to accept. All these years it has always felt as if I could reach you. It seemed so inevitable that I would, so right that we should find each other again and be together for what time was left to us in the same world. It seems wrong . . . terribly wrong . . . that we won't. Aletta's death was wrong in the same way.

(*Pause.*)

HELEN: What's the matter, Marius?

MARIUS: I am trying to go. It's not easy . . . trying to find the first moment of a life that must be lived out in the shadow of something that is terribly wrong.

HELEN: We're trying to say goodbye to each other, aren't we, Marius?

MARIUS: Yes, I suppose it had come to that. I never thought that was going to happen tonight, but I suppose there *is* nothing else left to say.

(MARIUS *starts to go. He sees* ELSA, *hesitates for a few seconds, but there is nothing to say to her either.*)

Be sure all the candles are out when you go to bed, Helen.

(*He pauses at the door.*)

I've never seen you as happy as this! There is more light in you than in all your candles put together.

(*He leaves. A silence follows his departure.* ELSA *eventually makes a move to start blowing out the candles.*)

HELEN: No, don't. I must do that.

(*From this point on* MISS HELEN *goes around the room putting out the candles, a quiet but deliberate and grave punctuation to what follows.*)

ELSA: Tell me about his wife.

HELEN: Her name was Aletta. Aletta Byleveld. I've only seen pictures of her. She must have been a very beautiful woman.

ELSA: What happened?

HELEN: Her death?

ELSA: Yes.

HELEN: All I know is that there was a long illness. And a very painful one. They never had any children. Marius was a bitter and lonely man when he first came to the valley. Why do you ask?

ELSA: Because he was, and most probably still is, in love with you.

HELEN: Elsa . . .

ELSA: Yes. I don't suppose I would have ever guessed it if it hadn't been for tonight. Like all good Afrikaners, he does a good job of hiding his feelings. But it is very obvious now.

HELEN: (*Agitated*) No, Elsie. When he used the word 'love' he meant it in the way . . .

ELSA: No, Helen. I'm not talking about the good shepherd's feelings for one of his flock. Marius Byleveld, the man, loves you Helen, the woman.

HELEN: What are you talking about? Look at me, Elsa. Look at my hands . . .

ELSA: You fool! Do you think that is what we see when we look at you? You heard him: 'There is more light in you than in all your candles put together.' And he's right. You are radiant. You can't be that naive and innocent, Helen!
(MISS HELEN *wants to deny it, but the validity, the possible truth, of what* ELSA *has said is very strong.*)
It's a very moving story. Twenty years of loving you in the disguise of friendship and professional concern for your soul.
(*There is an unnatural and forced tone to her voice.*)
Anyway, that's his problem, right, Helen? You did what you had to. In fact, you deserve a few bravos for your performance tonight. I'm proud of you. I told you that you never needed me. And you did more than just say no to him. You affirmed your right, as a woman . . .
(*Pause.*)
Do you love him? The way he loves you?
(MISS HELEN *thinks before speaking. When she does so there is no doubt about her answer.*)

HELEN: No, I don't.

ELSA: Just asking. You're also an Afrikaner. You could also be hiding your real feelings the way he did. That would make it an even better story! The two of you in this Godforsaken little village, each loving the other in secret!

HELEN: Are you all right, Elsa?

ELSA: No.

HELEN: What's wrong?

ELSA: It's my turn to be jealous.

HELEN: Of what?

ELSA: (*With a helpless gesture*) Everything. You and him . . . and, stupid as it may sound, I feel fucking lonely as well.

HELEN: You are jealous? Of us . . . Marius and me? With your whole life still ahead of you?

ELSA: Even that woman on the road has at least got a baby in her arms at this moment. She's got something, for Christ's sake! Mind you, it's cold out there now. It could be on her back again. She might have crawled out of her stormwater drain and started walking to keep warm.

HELEN: Leave that poor woman alone now, Elsa!

ELSA: She won't leave me alone, Helen!

HELEN: For all you know, she might have got a lift.

ELSA: (*Another unexpected flash of cruelty*) I hope not.

HELEN: (*Appalled*) Elsa! That is not you talking. You don't mean that.

ELSA: Yes, I do! A lift to where, for God's sake? There's no Mecca waiting for her at the end of that road, Helen. Just the rest of her life, and there won't be any glitter on that. The sooner she knows what the score really is, the better.

HELEN: Then think about the baby, Elsa.

ELSA: What the hell do you think I've been doing? Do you think I don't care? That baby could have been mine, Helen! (*Pause. Then a decision:*)
I may as well vomit it all out tonight. Two weeks after David left me I discovered I was pregnant. I had an abortion.
(*Pause.*)
Do you understand what I'm saying, Helen?

HELEN: I understand you, Elsa.

ELSA: I put an abrupt and violent end to the first real consequence my life has ever had.

HELEN: I understand, Elsa.
(*Pause.*)

ELSA: There is a little sequel to my story about giving that woman a lift. When I stopped at the turn-off and she got

76

out of the car, after I had given her what was left of my food and the money in my purse, after she had stopped thanking me and telling me over and over again that God would bless me, after all of that I asked her who she was. She said: 'My English name is Patience.' She hitched up the baby, tightened her *doek*, picked up her little plastic shopping bag and started walking. As I watched her walk away, measuring out the next eighty miles of her life in small steps, I wanted to scream. And about a mile further on, in the *kloof*, I did exactly that. I stopped the car, switched off the engine, closed my eyes and started to scream.

I think I lost control of myself. I screamed louder and longer than I have ever done in my life. I can't describe it, Helen. I hated her, I hated the baby, I hated you for dragging me all the way up here . . . and most of all I hated myself. That baby is mine, Helen. Patience is my sister, you are our mother . . . and I still feel fucking lonely.

HELEN: Then don't be so cruel to us. There were times tonight when I hardly recognized you. Why were you doing it?

ELSA: I wanted to punish us.

HELEN: For what? What have we done to deserve that?

ELSA: I've already told you. For being old, for being black, for being born . . . for being twenty-eight years old and trusting enough to jump. For our stupid helplessness.

HELEN: You don't punish people for that, Elsa. I only felt helpless tonight when I thought I had lost you.

ELSA: So what do you want me to do, Helen?

HELEN: Stop screaming.

ELSA: And cry instead?

HELEN: What is wrong with that? Is it something to be ashamed of? I wish I still could . . . not for myself . . . for you, Patience, her little baby. Was it a boy or a girl?

ELSA: I don't know. I'll never know.

(*Her moment of emotional release has finally come. She cries.* MISS HELEN *comforts her.*)

I'll be all right.

HELEN: I never doubted that for a moment.

ELSA: (*Total exhaustion*) God Almighty, what a day! I'm dead, Helen, dead, dead, dead . . .

HELEN: No, you're not. You're tired . . . and you've got every right and reason to be.

(*She fetches a blanket and puts it over* ELSA's *shoulders.*)

ELSA: I wasn't much of a help tonight, was I?

HELEN: You were more than that. You were a 'challenge'. I like that word.

ELSA: But we didn't solve very much.

HELEN: Nonsense! Of course we did. Certainly as much as *we* could. I *am* going to see a doctor and an optician, and Katrina . . . (*She remembers*) . . . or somebody else, will come in here a few times a week and help me with the house.

ELSA: My shopping list!

HELEN: It is as much as 'we' could do, Elsa. The rest is up to myself and, who knows, maybe it will be a little easier after tonight. I won't lie to you. I can't say that I'm not frightened any more. But at the same time I think I can say that I understand something now.

The road to my Mecca *was* one I had to travel alone. It was a journey on which no one could keep me company, and because of that, now that it is over, there is only me there at the end of it. It couldn't have been any other way.

You see, I meant what I said to Marius. This is as far as I can go. My Mecca is finished and with it – (*Pause*) I must try to say it, mustn't I? – the only real purpose my life has ever had.

(*She blows out a candle.*)

I was wrong to think I could banish darkness, Elsa. Just as I taught myself how to light candles, and what that means, I must teach myself now how to blow them out . . . and what that means.

(*She attempts a brave smile.*)

The last phase of my apprenticeship . . . and if I can get through it, I'll be a master!

ELSA: I'm cold.

HELEN: Cup of tea to warm you up and then bed. I'll put on the kettle.

ELSA: And I've got just the thing to go with it.
　　(*She goes into the bedroom alcove and returns with her toilet bag, from which she takes a small bottle of pills.*)
　　Valiums. The're delicious. I think you should also have one.
HELEN: (*All innocence*) So tiny! What are they? Artificial sweeteners?
　　(*The unintended and gentle irony of her question is not lost on* ELSA. *A little chuckle becomes a good laugh.*)
ELSA: That is perfect, Helen. Yes, they're artificial sweeteners.
HELEN: I don't know how I did it, but that laugh makes me as proud of myself as of any one of those statues out there.
　　(*She exits to put on the kettle.* ELSA *goes to the window and looks out at Mecca.* MISS HELEN *returns.*)
ELSA: Helen, I've just thought of something. You know what the real cause of all your trouble is? You've never made an angel.
HELEN: Good Heavens, no. Why should I?
ELSA: Because I think they would leave you alone if you did.
HELEN: The village doesn't need more of those. The cemetery is full of them . . . all wings and halos, but no glitter.
　　(*Tongue-in-cheek humour*) But if I did make one, it wouldn't be pointing up to heaven like the rest.
ELSA: No? What would it be doing?
HELEN: Come on, Elsa, you know! I'd have it pointing to the East. Where else? I'd misdirect all the good Christian souls around here and put them on the road to Mecca.
　　(*Both have a good laugh.*)
ELSA: God, I love you! I love you so much it hurts.
HELEN: What about trust?
　　(*Pause. The two women look at each other.*)
ELSA: Open your arms and catch me! I'm going to jump!

CURTAIN

DA